"Just Tell Me What To Do."
A Guide To Becoming The True YOU

Wendy Reese

Copyright © 2013 pitcbooks

All rights reserved.

ISBN:1493582968
ISBN-13:9781493582969

Insert dedication text here. Insert dedication text here. Insert dedication text here. Insert dedication text here. Insert dedication text here. Insert dedication text here. Insert dedication text here. Insert dedication text here. Insert dedication text here. Insert dedication text here.

Expand.
Breathe deeply.
In this moment,
no greater truth-
    you matter
    you are loved
    you are enough
All the scarcity and fear
just an illusion
a chance to feel
contrast to the infinite
You always have been
always will be
Divine
Free will to believe illusion
or not
Infinite has no words
only moments unfolding into the next
Welcome to MY playground
Exquisite, opulent, bliss
Join me.
Will you?
All it takes is "Yes!"
You don't have to know how.
Feel the bliss.
Breathe YOU in
and there you are with me
Just.
Like.
That.

CONTENTS

Just Tell Me What To Do!

"Why does this keep happening to me?"

"What is wrong with me?"

Have you ever asked either of those questions? I asked those questions one summer day and I was given the answer, "Because you do not like yourself, let alone love yourself, and until you do, you will keep repeating this lesson." For me, this was a cosmic two by four that hit me upside the head and rocked me to my core. You could say it woke me up. Pain is an incredible motivator for healing sometimes. I asked that voice of wisdom, "How?" No response. I thought, "Great. I'm hearing voices. It gives me wisdom followed by the silent treatment?" It did, however, give me the answer over the following three years through experiences, relationships, dark nights of the soul, and a lot of questions. I chose to dig in and explore honestly. There were many teachers on this path, some I knew personally and others were placed on my path to give me the tools I needed at the time. This guidebook is a manifesto of those lessons and tools.

The first part of this book is about exploration and understanding: who you are now, why you do what you do and feel what you feel. The human brain just loves to know "why." Awareness is the key that allows you to change. The second part of the book is about applying that awareness and making a shift. This is guidance into re-membering your essence, allowing the energy of Love to flow, and living your truest version of you in whatever epic way you choose. My Spiritual Director taught me that the best teachers do not necessarily answer your hardest questions, they ask you the right questions for you to discover your true answers. Use this part as a guide. What is interesting is that even though I have asked myself these questions many times, I always uncover something new.

For me the discovery has become an exciting adventure. I have taken all the questions and put them into a companion workbook to make it easier for you to explore. I know how hard it is to face your own stuff, take ownership, and make the shift. I also know how freaking amazing it is to be on the flip side of that place. That's why I am sharing this knowledge with you, because you matter. You are needed in this world. There is no one else out there who has your unique sacred contract and gifts. You are a spark of the Divine and that alone makes you good enough and worthy. So, are you ready for this? Let's do it.

Part 1: Past and Present: the great mystery of why you think what you think, feel what you feel, and do what you do.

Blocking the flow

One of my teachers in graduate school taught me two fundamental questions I have since learned to apply to almost everything, "So what?" and "Now what?" The "so what" I want to share with you is the "energy of Love." At our core or our essence, we are all the energy of Love. The energy is expressed uniquely by all; just as no two bodies are identical, no-two expressions of the energy of Love are identical. For example, I express mine through teaching yoga, writing, working with clients one-on-one, and leading workshops and classes. I have a friend who started a veteran-owned media company for veteran audiences. Another friend started a non-profit to feed the hungry and homeless. One of my best friends speaks honestly and candidly about the world as he sees it, speaking out about the injustices most people fail to see or are willing to discuss to avoid conflict. Another friend puts bodies back to their original blueprint. You can look all around you and see people who are expressing their Love through their words and actions.

Energetic Love is different than the emotion of love. Energetic Love is the energy that drives us to fight for what we believe in:
- to do superhuman feats in times of need
- to wake up and do it all over again, day in and day out because there are people counting on us, even when we are worn to the core
- to walk away even when you know in your soul it is the best choice; to sit next to a dying loved one and hold their hand while you muster all your strength not to fall apart
- to breathe rather than lash out; to find the strength to keep living when closing your eyes   and never waking up is more desirable.

That kind of Love and energy are always present, even when you cannot feel it or see evidence of its presence. Your purpose in life is rooted in this Love.

The energy of Love has a balance of light and shadow aspects. Duality of good and bad does not exist with these aspects, they simply are. Light qualities tend to be creative, life generating, and expansive. The shadow qualities tend to be constrictive and destructive. Because we are all energy, we have and we need both shadow and light aspects. Like antagonistic muscle groups, the shadow and light typically do not activate at the same time. In other words, if you are not creating, you are destroying. Bring awareness to your thought and actions. Are you building others up in your relationships or are you judging or tearing them down? In your conflicts are you generating solutions or are you digging a deeper hole? Are you more preoccupied with being right or being open to the infinite possibilities? We have the power to create: our lives, beliefs, stories, romances, art, friendships, meaning, ideas, even other lives when conceiving a child. The Divine (the higher power, God, Allah, whatever you call it), creative source is within us, experiencing *through* us. Being created in the image of the Divine, *all* the emotions we feel, are Divine. Through free will, you get to express your energy of Love uniquely.

You have the freedom to disconnect from the flow of the energy of Love. Growth does not happen in the easy, carefree times. Those are times for rest, renewal, gratitude, and soul memory building. Growth usually happens in times of challenge. Disconnecting from the energy of Love creates suffering for the soul. Hurt people hurt; they hurt themselves, others, or both. Hurt people are not broken. They do not need to be fixed. I feel this is worth repeating - Hurt people are hurt, *not broken*. They need to heal and reconnect. The disconnection creates a spiritual disability, not so different from a developmental disability, which will impact all areas of life until the hurt is released and flow is reconnected.

Though it has a significant purpose, disconnecting seems like a counterintuitive thing to do. You are a Divine, infinite being. In order to experience the Divine qualities more fully, you made a sacred contract, or spiritual agreement, for your life. Likely, you have no recollection of what you chose for your sacred contract. In order to experience the totality of the Divine expression of Love, you have to know the shadow as well as the light aspects. These qualities are simply energy, two sides of the same coin. In the moment that you cease to experience the energy of Love, for whatever reason, it hurts. The pain created by that challenge is what breaks the connection. The deeper the disconnection, the greater the opportunity to grow. Have you ever seen a stream or a river become blocked? The water backs up, still trying to flow, until it bursts through or reroutes. This is what happens in humans with the energy of Love. The soul is like the water. It will continue to push, often by recreating experiences in order to harmonize and heal, or reroute by surrendering and creating "new,,"" authentic beliefs and stories in order to reconnect. The disconnection is painful. Your mind knows pain is what gets attention far more than pleasure, so the body uses it to drive you to do something about the situation, either heal or numb the pain.

No matter how deeply you bury a hurt or try to repress the pain, your subconscious knows innately that you are the energy of Love. The subconscious works with the soul to do everything it can to make sense of the hurt in order to reconnect. The subconscious brings people and situations into your life over and over in order to try to understand and heal the pain. You have to remember (read that as re-member) your essence in order to flow again.

It took me 35 years from when my energy was disconnected until I knew I loved myself and was living as authentically as I knew how. In those 35 years, I attracted so many opportunities to heal that pain of disconnection. I destroyed many relationships, gave away so many opportunities, and hated myself which only deepened the separation of Love. I don't want anyone else to have to experience what I witnessed in myself, family, friends, and clients. I am not so naive to believe that if we could all get to a place where our Love energy is flowing that we will have a utopian society, there will be world peace, and we'll all hold hands and sing "Kumbaya." We all have some Divine qualities we want to experience more fully in this lifetime and to do that, we have to be challenged which is often uncomfortable at best and horrifically painful at worst. My goal is to help you lift the veils and allow the energy of Love to flow, so that the day-to-day stuff doesn't have to be suffering and when the real challenges emerge, you know how to handle them as effectively and efficiently as possible, bringing yourself back to center as quickly as possible. I want to help you experience this life as the great adventure and love affair rather than just doing what you can to get by. Survival mode is necessary from time to time; living in that mode all time sucks. Destruction is sometimes useful to clear the stuck spaces that are not in harmony with the energy of Love. You have to be willing to feel into the discomfort and pain of being stuck deeply in order to finally say, "Enough!" and be willing to shift into a different energy.

Sometimes a person can be so disconnected that they believe they can no longer reconnect. They feel "broken." The language such a person uses is limiting, "I'm not good enough," "I'll never..." and "I'm not worthy." I don't buy into the idea of a person being "broken," nor do I believe that the experiences that come from their pain warrant a mental health label. I agree that there are legitimate mental illnesses that come from chemical imbalances and other genetic dispositions. Based on observing my clients, more often than not, depression, anxiety, or phobias come from a deep pain. This pain stems from a need that has not been met, the fear of never wanting to feel that pain again, or from the faulty mental belief of not being good enough, worthy, and/or lovable. That is a painful place to live. It is reinforced daily by messages distributed by advertising and entertainment that imply you're not enough until you have or use their product. Labeling or medicating the hurt does not heal the wounds, reconnect to body and soul, help with accepting the experiences, or release the trapped energy inside the armor. At best, it numbs, rationalizes, or justifies the pain. These painful experiences are necessary to touch the soft spots under your protective outer shell and behind your guarded walls surrounding your heart center, alerting you that disharmony exists. You chose to stay in the limitations and illusions or you can surrender and return to the flow.

The Role of Energy

Energy is a dynamic quality. All beliefs, values, needs, and actions begin with thoughts. If I cut you open, I could not see a thought, belief, value, or need inside you, yet you believe they exist. Thoughts, illusionary as they are, become things. Thoughts carry their own energy because they are anchored to emotions. Here's an example. Someone enters a room and, without ever saying a word, you know that they are angry. In fact, the angrier they are, the more you physically try to remove yourself from their proximity as a defense mechanism. However, if the same person walked in and, again without words, you could see that the person was happy, maybe even giddy; you find yourself leaning in closer, trying to find out what is happening. You are naturally drawn to the happy person, while the angry person repels you. Emotions are energy.

There are high vibrating energies and low vibrating energies. High vibrations generate emotions that make you feel physically lighter: happy, sexy, desirable, funny, and peaceful. Low vibrating energies are heavy: anger, depression, fear, rage, and anxiety. Interestingly, it is physically impossible to mask the outward expression of almost all of these emotions, even for the most skilled at deception. The brain knows the facial expressions. Anyone witnessing the expressions will know how you feel, even if only on a subconscious level. Without words, you give people permission to treat you a certain way simply because of the way you are thinking. Even if you think you are brilliant at pretending to be happy or confident, people instinctively know the truth, perhaps without even being able to articulate why.

"Fake it 'til you make it" holds some merit. Just by changing your posture or facial expression your brain will react and begin to change how you feel. However, it is not a good long-term strategy because you have to take action to heal the roots and the layers of pain. You cannot always feel happy. There are many emotions that exist and all are appropriate when felt and released. Doing so begins with awareness.

What you resist will persist. The persistence is the focus of your energy that attracts more of the same energies, situations, people, and emotions. Joy, happiness, courage, compassion and empathy exist within you even if you are feeling darkness (fear, anger, rage, anxiety, or sadness). You have the capacity to experience both, even if both sides are not obviously present. When you resist something, you put your body into a place of fight or flight (we will discuss this in chapter 8). You become your biggest threat to a positive existence because this begins a cycle of being both a victim and an aggressor towards yourself, the very cycle that keeps you stuck in a place of discomfort, disease, and suffering.

The law of conservation of energy states that energy can neither be created nor destroyed; it can only be transformed from one state into another. Through your choices, you are responsible for how you act and react every moment of the day. Everything is a choice and has an associated energetic vibrational charge. Even ignoring the exchange is a choice. Ignoring does not make something disappear. The exchange is still taking place. Giving up your own needs and desires to make someone else happy eventually creates an unworthiness belief in you that transforms into a low vibrating energy, which attracts more opportunities to confirm or change that belief.

Desensitization and dehumanization are a by-products of disconnection. Because the energy of Love is still alive, perhaps deeply buried or disconnected, the call of that energy creates a deep sense of shame and guilt for not being in harmony or in the flow. All thoughts, actions, and relationships are infused with the shame and guilt. The pendulum then swings to the extreme of judgment and condemnation. Suffering ensues while a crusade to be right and pain-free marches on. Disconnection creates a place of limitations. Connection allows you to be limitless. You have a simple choice: be limited or limitless.

When your energy ceases to be exchanged, the disconnect makes you feel like a refugee in a foreign land; you don't belong there but you can't get home either. James Welch writes in *Winter in the Blood*, "Coming home was not so easy anymore... The distance I felt came not from country or people; it came from within me. I was as distant from myself as a hawk from the moon." Until you can touch the soft spots, the best you can do is attempt assimilation. You begin to settle. You get by with what you have, even though you know it is not right, not home, and not you.

You have blocked the flow of love and suffered the consequences. Now is the time to unblock that flow. To return you to yourself, your mind needs to understand the spaces that the illusions and limitations that you were creating. Awareness allows different choices to be made. As you do, you eventually look back, laugh, and think, "I can't believe I did that to myself!" The journey evolves from a struggle to an incredible adventure.

"I"dentity

Though children may not understand why, they know when their needs are not being met. In that moment, there is a disconnection to the flow of Love's energy. The conscious starts wrestling with the question, "Why?" Children personalize cause and effect. There is no memory of the sacred contract of experiencing the Divine qualities in their totality, both shadow and light. There is no memory of making energetic agreements of who would help them with this process. They do not understand that blockage stems from adults inadequacies to provide the energy in that moment. The child's interpretations of the block, "It's not safe to be me" shapes how the child utilizes actions and reactions to avoid the pain. If you experienced this as a child, you likely created stories and rapidly formed beliefs that molded future experiences, especially how to "be" in order to be accepted.

As children grow, they imitate their caretakers because that is who will keep them alive with food, water, and shelter. The child, therefore, wants to keep the grown-up happy. Happy brings approval. "That's my boy!" or "That's my little girl!" are compliments bestowed for getting a tradition right. Yet, the soul still calls out for authenticity even when it is at odds with what the adult desires the child to be. If the child follows the inauthentic path, they will wrestle with a deep seeded guilt and shame over the longing and likely failed attempts at being authentic. If you are a man, you may have developed beliefs that you are supposed to be authoritative, strong, disciplined, a problem solver, and competent. For women, characteristics such as being strong, independent, capable, nurturing, quiet, feminine, cooperative, or supportive are expected. Meanwhile, your authentic being longs to be expressed uniquely and has both polarities (and their expressions) of masculinity and femininity. Your authentic being possesses a full gamut of emotions, a balance between shadow and light, creative and destructive.

The reality is that the polarities of masculine and feminine exist within all of us. After all, you are genetically made from a man and woman, so you have each sex's DNA within you. You have space within your container of a body for all of it. Embracing both makes you no less or no more of one gender or the other. Embracing both makes you powerful and balanced. However, society forces people into gender roles. It is the first question asked of expecting parents, "Is it a boy or a girl?" If you are a boy and not athletic, you are called weak or a geek. If you do not learn the way education is structured for the norm, you are considered stupid or learning disabled. If you have had to fight to be heard, you are often labeled as a problem child. Little boys who like to put on dresses and wear make-up or play with dolls are labeled weak, sissy, or gay. While a girl who is strong and athletic is considered a dyke or butch. If she is confident and assertive in her career, she is labeled a bitch. A norm of "wrong" is imposed. Without a loving support system, the child begins to learn to either repress their authenticity because they might jeopardize acceptance. A child quickly learns that being authentic is not safe or receives judgment around authenticity, creating a sense of unworthiness.

Children learn the painful lessons of speaking their authentic truth at a young age. Kids are unfiltered and pure. They speak the truth as they see it. Only when adults start to teach wrong from right, do the filters that lead to false beliefs develop. I am a sass, always have been. Though I now have an understanding of when it is inappropriate and the ability to authentically communicate in other ways. I can remember standing my ground, sometimes under my breath, of course. "What did you say?" an angry parent would glare down at me. Bowing my head to avoid eye contact, I would mumble, "Nothing." I also experienced the question, "Are you talking back to me?" on a regular basis. I am not the only child who responded "no" when "yes" was the truth. I just didn't like the punishment that followed if I were to speak what I really felt. In school, I spent a lot of time in the hallway getting "swats" (it was Oklahoma in the 70's and 80's and corporal punishment was accepted and utilized). Being spanked did not alter my Divine, infinite being. It gave me pause to wonder why it was not safe to be my light and Love.

At a young age you learn to say "yes" when you really want to say "no" because you don't want to hurt feelings, disappoint, be abandoned, rejected, punished or unaccepted. Parents who are not fluent in the language of needs utilize guilt. "You don't want to make Mommy sad, do you?" or "You don't want to make Daddy angry." We say "no" when we mean "yes" out of fear, too. Everyone has a deep desire that evolves into a need for belonging, for wanting safety and security. Ultimately, you abandon, betray, and reject your own essence when you stray from authenticity. You form patterns and cycles. As a dear friend once said, "It's everyone's fault and no one is to blame."

Teenagers seek to express the energy of Love uniquely. This is in complete odds with their deep need for belonging. Teens push their boundaries or hide behind images that give them a sense of belonging. They push and pull. They try to figure it out, get hurt, self-protect, tentatively reach forward again, and keep trying, maybe. Some don't because they can't imagine experiencing humiliation again so they become cautious or give up. And some are so deeply wounded that it impacts them for the rest of their life. They may manage to be functional; however, they put on emotional armor while under the surface fear and rage dominate and silently accumulate. Subconsciously, they carry these lessons that shape their perceived identity into adulthood.

Have you ever wondered who you are and how you got to where you are? You look around at the people in your life, your job, your finances, or your health and it makes no sense. How did it get this way? Worse, you don't know how to change it. You feel awful, even if the job or relationship looks fine, maybe even ideal, from an outsider's perspective. Maybe you are carrying extra weight and though you receive expert advise on nutrition and exercise, your heart knows you have been feeding more than biological hunger. The advice goes unheard. In your heart, you know something is wrong, but you can't identify what it is.

When authenticity is denied, a slow process of spiritual death begins. The process builds resentment because killing your essence is counterintuitive and your subconscious *knows* that and fights it. You never forget all the times you were asked to be inauthentic. You know intuitively when you are not being loved or accepted unconditionally. In order to protect from the pain, you create emotional armor, stories, and beliefs with each inauthentic, hurtful experience. The layers of emotional armor get thicker. The walls grow higher. In turn, resentments begin to build until the bridges to healing the relationship, the job, whatever the case may be, are burned as you fight your way back to authenticity. Some people will suffer through the resentment because they were taught to stick to their commitments at any price. In both cases, the outcomes are truly tragic and painful for all involved because the flow of Love's energy is blocked, unable to connect to other's energy, unable to offer its unique gifts unconditionally. Experiencing that disconnection causes suffering.

The masks you wear

Armor was traditionally used as a mechanism to protect from harm during battle. Now you employ emotional armor, in theory, to protect from feeling pain. The desire to avoid pain can be temporarily met through food, adrenaline, alcohol, drugs, sex, *anything* to stop the pain for a bit. People bury themselves in the lives of others through television or sports because it is easier than living their own life, stepping into their own greatness, and living authentically. Some people bury themselves in work in an attempt to create an ideal life with enough prestige, possessions, and image to keep them and their partner "happy." Some bury themselves in food, cigarettes, alcohol or drugs to control the emptiness, loneliness, or pain. There are so many ways to attempt a sense of control. Some people attempt to avoid their pain by trying to numb through anti-depressants, anti-anxiety and sleeping medications. After a long enough period, the blessed numbness just happens, creating a balance that allows daily functioning. If you stay protected long enough, you may forget how to feel *anything* except the negative feelings.

Eventually though, the armor becomes a curse when feelings are replaced by numbness. This goes against everything the soul wants, needs, and desires. The soul is here in your body to experience life completely as a Divine, infinite being. The soul is a tenacious little thing, and it will fight like hell for survival. The soul wants to feel everything, shadow *and* light, because those are its guides. So eventually the pendulum will swing in the opposite direction. You try to feel *something*, this time pushing the limits to get beyond the numbness because, really, if you can't feel anything, then what is the point of being alive?

In the movie *Fight Club* they beat the hell out of one another just to feel alive. Maybe it is adrenaline you choose in order to feel alive. Maybe you need high-risk behavior to provide that high. Or maybe you choose drama and play the victim in order to get attention. If you push hard enough, you bring those very needs to the surface that if unmet cause pain. The warning signals turn on with sirens blazing. Danger! Potential ouch! Turn it off! Start the numbing! Then the pendulum swings back to attempt to numb. Perhaps this is the best description for suffering; a constant swinging between all or nothing, and neither solves the problem of unhealed pain.

Sometimes when the soul calls for you to step into your authenticity, fear overrides the message. Instead of heeding the call, you try to find a way to appease it as you struggle to be strong, independent, and in control. You hold yourself back and then wonder why you can't move forward, reach your dreams, heal your body and mind. There is only so much you can do to hide your authenticity behind the armor. The armor reinforces guilt, shame, loneliness, feeling of inadequacy, and pain; barriers to liberating authenticity. Every time you look in the opposite direction when faced with injustice, every time you shrink back from authenticity out of fear, every time you do not say what you mean, and every time you settle for less than your heart desires, the armor grows a little more with every fight or avoidance of the fight. It may protect you from pain, but it keeps you from healing and creates a vicious cycle. The armor is an illusion.

Control

The need to prove strength, control, and independence is all about protecting against vulnerability. The Latin root of the word vulnerability is vulnerare, which means "to wound". The irony is that the very armor used to protect you against being wounded is the exact thing that prevents your wounds from healing. As long as you hold your hands tightly gripped into a fist, clinging to the need to be in control, strong, without need of help from anyone, you cannot grow because you cannot receive. You cannot be hugged (well, you can, but it won't really touch you in the way you need). You cannot feel all the emotions and use them as guides for growth and healing. The tension atrophies your essence or soul. In other words, as long as you want to stay strong, in control, and independent, you will remain stuck.

How can anyone ever be in control of *anything*? There are just too many variables. With almost seven billion people in this world, each doing their own thing, dictated by their values and beliefs that are influenced by families, friends, society, and religions, how can you control anything other than your own self? Add to that mix your own actions and reactions, that are often deeply subconscious and therefore essentially out of your perceived control. Control is an illusion.

You cannot control another person. I have a dear friend who lives in a country occupied by a government that has made it illegal to even talk about, let alone, practice her traditional faith. My friend said on numerous occasions, "You can control what we do to a point, but you can never control what is in our heart and mind." It's true. In abusive, manipulating situations, force controls through fear. The aggressor may even be fooled into believing it is a form of respect. You may have engaged at some level in this behavior or been on the receiving end. This level of false identity is destructive on an exponential level. Ironically, the weakest and most insecure individuals also use it by playing the victim-entitlement role. The more out-of-control you feel, the more you will try to compensate. Sometimes when I feel out-of-control, I feel like the rattlesnake that is backed into a corner. I will do what it takes to regain control. I can see this happening and I have learned to try to sit with this sense and ask myself, "What am I trying to control? Is there something inauthentic that I need to release? Do I fear being hurt? Am I feeling not good enough?" This brings me back to my center to make wiser choices in the moment.

The out-of-control feeling will appear when you don't know how to meet your needs and you seek others to meet them. You give away your power when you rely on others to meet your needs. Expecting someone else to meet your needs is unrealistic and unfair because they most likely do not know what you need. I have witnessed far too many people give their power away. So worried about rejection, they hand their power to others. Think you don't give away your power? Single men give away their power to potential mates by not planning dates, just going along with whatever that date wants because he does not want to "screw it up" or "disappoint." Married men and women swallow their voice to keep the peace because it is easier and cheaper than risking a divorce or because they are afraid of being alone. People remain in jobs they hate, belittled by their employers, and resenting their co-workers. Truth is, being anything less than authentic is settling. Giving other people control over your life gives you the opportunity to call yourself a victim. You are not a true victim, though, only one of your own choice.

Feeling out-of-control can be paralyzing. Thoughts like, "Who am I to think I can change anything?" or, "How could I ever get that big project done when it is only me?" take over the mind. All the fret and fright leads to nothing happening. You give your power away to the unknown. The reality is a baby learns how to walk by first rolling, then rocking, on to crawling, followed by pulling up to standing, and finally taking a wobbly step before falling down. Like a baby learning to walk, you take one small action step towards your goal and you keep taking baby steps. If you start exercising just 10 minutes a day, by the end of the week you will have more energy. If you start eating nutritiously and cut out the junk, you will lose weight. Does the energy or weight loss happen overnight? Of course not! However, even the biggest, scariest, most global problems can be impacted by every person taking one small step towards a more balanced resolution.

Routine and control are often mistaken for one another. People like routines. They are safe. Get up, get ready, go to work, go to lunch, go back to work, go home, have dinner, relax, go to bed, rinse and repeat. Sure, there could be more to the routine, but that's the general skeleton wouldn't you say? When you break-up with someone or you leave your job, you do not experience the devastation as much because you have already decided to alter your routine and adapt a new one. However, when someone breaks-up with you, when you are fired, or when someone hurts you, *they* alter your routine. You feel out-of-control.

When you say, "I don't ever want to feel that kind of pain again," you shut down and close off any opportunities you perceive could possibly create pain. This gives the the mind permission to do what it can to protect you. You protect against an unknown enemy and project that role onto anyone that could potentially hurt you. Still, the longing to connect to the energy of Love exists and keeps tugging at your every fiber of being. It becomes a tug-of-war between ego and soul. The fear of the pain is so great that the armor thickens a little more, keeping out the pain and suppressing wants, desires, and needs.

As humans, we don't want the world to know we are capable of feeling pain or fear. Aren't we all, in some way, afraid of being found out to be a fraud? To feel fear creates vulnerability. The belief is that if you are vulnerable, you will appear weak, be taken advantage of or manipulated, leading to being hurt. When you feel insecure and try to pretend you are strong and in control, you project aggressiveness, even if that is not your intention, which makes the person on the receiving end defensive. Their defensiveness in turn signals to you that it is not safe to be vulnerable. Even if you are not vulnerable, you're going to get hurt. Think about people who go on stage in front of strangers to share their story or wisdom. Do you consider them weak? Most people consider that brave. So what is the difference between their courageous vulnerability and that which you view as weak within yourself? Vulnerability builds connection, depth, and trust.

This is life. You're going to feel pain. Embrace it. Use it. That pain can be an enormously powerful tool if you allow it. Under your armor, the calm, small voice of the soul, deep within the body, though numbed, is still gnawing at you. I felt that at the start of my journey when my ego screamed louder than my whispering essence. My soul clawed its way to my attention. I was trying so hard to be "good enough" that I lost track of the fact that I have always been more than enough.

Strength comes from vulnerability and authenticity. When you surrender, really surrender, you just might find what you needed all along. The armor you wear now is an identity that you have created to protect yourself from pain. That identity is not you. You know it, too, on a deep, cellular level. It is the constant, typically low-grade friction that keeps you repeating patterns, self-sabotaging, and pushing yourself into bigger, better, faster and stronger: more money, a bigger house, a cooler car, a hotter partner. Those things can ease the discomfort from the friction for a moment, but never long-term.

Uncovering / Peeling off the masks

One of my favorite questions is, "Who are you?" Stop reading and take a moment to really think about this. Go beyond all the labels, identities, and roles. I get that you are a man or a woman, a son or daughter, a friend, a lover. Maybe you are a brother or sister, cousin, uncle or aunt, father or mother, employee or employer, hard worker, athlete, thinker, poet, artist, moral and upstanding citizen. Cool. All those rock. At your core, though, who *are* you?

It took a long time for me to figure this out about myself. I used to identify with all sorts of labels, roles, and expectations. It was exhausting. I used to think I had to be strong, independent, and in control. I fought hard to be that and I tried to convince everyone I was. I sacrificed to maintain that identity. I was so scared someone would see me for who I really was. My false identity seemed brash, aggressive, cold, arrogant, untouchable, and not at all connected to what I really felt. For a long time I didn't know who I was and why I was here. I felt lost and out of control and I didn't want anyone to know. I was embarrassed and ashamed because everyone thought I was so together. I did what it took to keep up the charade.

This false identity we create takes us down a lonely road of dishonesty, greed, and hatred. You can never have enough when you are trying to fill the void and the pain of your soul being buried. When you are seeking joy, peace, and love outside of yourself, you can never attain enough to quench that thirst. You see in others what you really want and need so you project your own self-disdain onto them. Hating is easier than facing the unmet need inside you. False identity is layered in dishonesty. Every lie propagates another lie until it is difficult to differentiate truth from fiction.

The fear of being discovered and judged for your authenticity is so great that it is easier to try to be what you think others want you to be. It may work for a bit. Long term, though, it is a lousy strategy. Threats to the image you portray can instigate battles. "I'll show you" and "I'm right, you're wrong" are merely examples of defense mechanisms. Unfortunately, few people ever investigate why they have their particular identity, all the while defending it and creating stronger armor. The irony is that when you choose to live authentically, you can step into a place of vulnerability and gain your strength because there is nothing to fear, no lies to remember, no skeletons to hide, no one to invest energy in pleasing at the cost of your soul. You can experience the array of emotions, use them as guides, and be able to process through without attachment to any one particular emotion. They become your trusted companions, confidants, and mentors.

When you are numbed and protected, sleepwalking through life, you find yourself wondering, "Is this it?" No, this isn't it. This isn't the best it will ever be, either. Likewise, it may not be the worst. All the armor and false identities have created beliefs that now have to be re-examined as we will do in the next chapter. The process takes time, commitment, and even courage because you have brought people into your life to help you with your sacred contract. As you start to evaluate your beliefs, you will experience friction from some of the same people who helped you create your beliefs. Just remember that the challenge brings growth. Believe it.

Beliefs and Stories

I took an Introduction to Philosophy class years ago. The instructor asked, "What are your basic beliefs?" I thought to myself, "Oh that's easy," then proceeded to sit there waiting for something, *anything* to come to mind. I had no idea what I really believed. The few things I *could* identify, I had no idea why I believed. It took me *two years* of exploration to really shape and define my beliefs.

Have you ever really looked at what you believe and why? A belief is the acceptance of a truth, trust, and/or opinion. When I ask my clients and students about their beliefs, they immediately go to virtues. While there is nothing wrong with those, they are instilled in us from our earliest days. Who says those beliefs are worthy of *your* acceptance of their truth? Who says they aren't merely an opinion? Who says they are worthy of your trust? Many beliefs only consist of the light aspects, completely denying the energy of shadow aspects, so they are not whole.

Let's play here. What do you believe? Do you believe you are good enough? Do you believe you are worth billions of dollars even if your bank account does not reflect that value? Bill Gates net worth is over $65 billion. Aren't you worth that? Is he any better, creative, lovable, ethical, or moral than you? Do you believe you are gorgeous? Do you believe you are smart enough? Do you believe you could change the world? Why or why not? Do you believe you could ever believe in anything so much you would die for it? Do you believe that there is something, anything wrong with you? Do you believe you are not worthy? Incapable? Inadequate? Do you believe you matter? Do you believe you're alone or incomplete? Powerless?

Children are experts at body language and energy because it is the first thing they learn before they learn to speak. As a child, you picked up on body language from time to time and realized whatever you were doing or saying was not okay in the moment. It may have had nothing to do with your words and behaviors, rather the adult you picked up the cue from having a disconnection. In that moment, you feared being ostracized and pulled back. There is a cycle that happens in your mind; you experience something, painful or pleasurable, and your mind makes a mental bookmark. You create a belief around the thoughts of that experience; you like it or you don't like it. These become emotional triggers. If your need was met and you liked the experience, you felt a pleasant or positive emotion the next time you experienced something similar. If your need was not met, you felt pain or discomfort, you decided you didn't like it, the next time you experienced something similar, you had a shadowy emotional charge.

Your mind makes a map for future reference. You then develop a reference library of maps. The maps become your filters and views (beliefs) of reality. There is a place in your brain called the orbitofrontal cortex that is important in signaling punishment and reward. It reads your mind's maps. It cues the emotional triggers in order to motivate you to approach and take further action, to freeze and gather more data, or to run from the undesirable experience. Your mind is efficient and starts to read these maps faster and faster each time they are engaged. The problem with that is that the situation may not be identical, though the mind tells the body to react before it knows for sure. Simultaneously, you create stories to make sense of or alleviate the pain. The more you tell the story, especially to yourself, the more entrenched the belief.

What happens when your beliefs are built upon the foundation that you are not good enough, not worthy, and not lovable? Your essence knows better and your soul will keep trying to make you believe it by attracting opportunities to harmonize and heal. This is

29

where most people become stuck. It feels self-sabotaging because you repeat behaviors over and over without a sense of why. In order to break the patterns, you have to start exploring the roots. Are these beliefs helping or hindering you from growing and healing? Are your beliefs getting you any closer to being happy, healthy, and authentic?

Believing that you are fat, lazy, and weak-willed makes being healthy a challenge. Believing you are unlovable is in direct conflict with your essence. Believing that the world is a scary place, every man for himself, and there simply isn't enough to go around, hinders your ability to appreciate what you have or allow you to deeply connect with others. The emotional triggers stimulated by the beliefs prepare your body for fight or flight. This pattern goes from an emotional response to a physiological level, as it reinforces the map your brain uses to guide you. Have you ever heard, "I am my own worst enemy"? You make the enemy as you are constantly entering a fight or flight mode not because of an actual threat, rather because of your own beliefs. You *are* the enemy!

For years I believed that everyone I loved would die, leave, or shut down. I believed it was my fault in some way, that I was not good enough or worthy enough and if I was just a little better I could change everything. I would play a game of push and pull where I would get close to breaking through and then I would shutdown, pull away, or lash out. I kept the cycle alive until I realized all this behavior stemmed from a story I created as a way to protect myself. I learned a life-changing lesson; I could create a new story based on facts. Your ego will resist this because it has used your stories to "protect" you for so long. It will make you believe that a new story is not possible. That is a lie. The only challenge is being willing to believe and say, "yes" to creating an authentic story.

When I experienced the moment of realization that I neither loved nor liked myself, I wondered how I could change that. I remember hearing very clearly, and then almost like a slideshow, seeing in my mind's eye, the faces of friends who loved and supported me through good times and bad. You have at least one person in your life that knows you; what you have done or have failed to do, your dreams and insecurities. This person knows what a jerk you can be sometimes. They have also seen you be big-hearted. They know you *and* they still love you. If this person can know all that and still love you, you can learn how to love you, too. Embrace your shadows and poor decisions as they have served their purpose in your growth. Holding on to your hurt for the sake of validating your unworthiness keeps you stuck in a victim cycle. What is done is done. Only when you embrace and accept them, you can you move beyond shame and guilt.

Roots of beliefs

The heart knows which beliefs are true and which are false. Under the weight of the fear of being hurt, the body begins to physically wrap itself around the heart, shoulders cave inward, the spine changes alignment, and the head sinks downward, all of this to protect the soft spot where the unmet needs reside. Still, the lessons will keep coming, gently urging you to open your heart, meet the needs, and heal the wounds. Opening your heart is essentially exposing the heart and exploring your needs. This is also an excellent way to explore your beliefs.

Do you know what it is to feel connection and empathy? This is the deepest wound for most of us. You want to feel accepted, appreciated, close, a sense of belonging, respect, and that you matter. In your relationships, you want to feel a sense of affection, consideration, consistency, humor, intimacy, and trust. You want to feel heard and you want to know what is really going on inside those you care about because you want to make life better for those people. You want to feel a part of the tribe or team. You want to have a sense of community. You want to have fun. You wonder if those you let in will be there for you when you need them. Can they be trusted? This is the place where many people feel "abandoned."

As a child, when these needs go unmet, you develop a sense of unworthiness, of being unlovable, of being not good enough. You develop thoughts such as, "If I were _____, I could be accepted, appreciated, and belong." Unfortunately, trying to be enough is not only impossible it completely goes against your essence, creating suffering and disconnection. You are already enough. These feelings of not being enough are deeply rooted in the subconscious. We are not even aware of how they affect us on a daily basis. The need for connection and empathy drives many of your decisions. You create stories that validate your beliefs, help you to connect to others with similar unmet needs, and keep you perpetually in a victim role.

Examining Beliefs

What evidence exists to contradict your beliefs? As you become more aware of what you believe and why, what behaviors would you like your beliefs to support? If you have a hard time communicating, perhaps the behaviors are being open, honest, authentic, able to listen and be heard. If you want to feel loved, you must first believe you are worthy and lovable, so what behaviors would support that? Defining the desired behaviors is a way of creating intention. Ultimately, successful completion of the intention develops inner strength, character, and power.

Beliefs filter everyday interactions. When you know you are moving into a state of conflict, the brain scans the maps and determines whether to be on the offense or defense based on whether it is painful or pleasurable. Instead, take a breath and reflect. What are you feeling right now? Name the emotion (a list of emotions and feelings are included in the appendix). Where do you feel it in your body? What does it feel like? What is causing you to feel this way? Dig deeper and look for your deepest, most heartfelt longing. What do you need? Ask yourself what thoughts, words or actions could increase or decrease the intensity of both the undesirable and the desired feeling? This simple awareness is powerful and can change the course of the conflict quickly. Write these questions on a piece of paper and keep it with you for a week. You will be surprised how often you use it.

I remember processing those questions with a client who had just broken up with his significant other. He said his biggest problem was moving past the relationship and wondering if he had made the right choice. I asked him what he felt when he thought about this problem. The emotions identified were fear and anger and he felt it in his chest and stomach. These emotions were tight and heavy. Identifying the cause of these emotions was a greater challenge. Ultimately, he felt like a fool for leaving and feared ultimately never living his ideal life in a loving, supportive relationship. I took it a step further and asked, "What need was served by making the decision to leave?" My client shared that he felt he was suffocating in the relationship, unheard, misunderstood, and lost, no longer knowing who he was anymore. I asked, "What would increase or decrease the intensity of the constriction and heaviness around the heart and belly?" My client had never thought about that. I processed through several scenarios, asking if they increased or decreased the sensation in his body:

>Going back to your partner and working together on
>communication and autonomy;
>Starting fresh;
>Being able to speak your truth in other areas of your life;
>Identifying your needs and being able to ask for them;
>Feeling loved.

With each suggestion, he paid attention to his body and how it felt. My client realized several key issues: the loss of his authenticity, not feeling loved and supported, and the lack of communication. At the surface, he believed he would never be loved again and would never have another loving partnership. Going a little deeper, he discovered he did not really believe he was worthy of a loving relationship. This false belief was keeping him stuck. We worked together to help him, literally, re-member he is the energy of Love and begin to let that energy flow. He started creating a new story based on facts.

Going even deeper to understand the layers around your beliefs can stop the cycles of repeating the same lesson. What is your true reason for what you do or say? Here is an example that happened with a friend of mine. One day, I made an observation. My friend's brother had brought my friend's dog to walk at the park where my friend and I were exercising with his sons. My friends' attention was more on the dog than his boys. The boys were doing something that was potentially dangerous. I pointed it out, he made a momentary acknowledgement, and then promptly returned his attention back to the dog. Later, when I shared my observation that he seemed to care more about the dog than his boys in that moment, he took what I said and changed the word "care" to "love" in his mind, completely changing the context of what I said. I know this man loves his sons very deeply and would go to the ends of the earth for them. I also know he loves his dog. In that moment, knowing him as well as I did, his priorities felt out of balance to me. He responded to my observation by telling me why he was so focused on the dog and that my observation was incorrect. I let it go. The next day, he brought it up again. I started asking him to tell me what need of his was not being met that it caused him to think all night and into the next morning about my observation. He tried to deflect. He blamed me for complicating a simple issue and having a compulsive need to be right. His reaction to me was a projection of his deepest internal fear.

He cared about my opinion of him and felt that he had failed me in some way. The deeper issue had nothing to do with me. It had more to do with his fear of being like his parents and not meeting the needs of his children and of needing to be viewed as strong, in control, and independent. He feared that he was not a good enough father or in some way would fail his boys. His innermost, heartfelt reason for bringing it up was the need for validation and approval. Of course I could validate and approve him as a person and it would make him feel better temporarily. Yet, until he could validate and approve himself, he would always search for that outside himself, subconsciously creating situations that confirmed the belief that he was not "enough," and hitting the proverbial brick wall.

Fear comes from sensory inputs derived from learned experiences. Underneath the fear is a longing for your highest self. That fear has protected you from the pain of unmet needs. When you can identify the fear and identify the needs, you can break the painful patterns that keep you stuck. You can identify ways to meet the needs, and thereby create new beliefs. Working into the roots is about developing your instinct. When you can feel your way through an experience, you use the energy of Love to create rather than continuing the cycles of destruction and pain, shame, or guilt and that, my friend, is liberation from the tyranny of self.

Feelings

From an early age, we are taught that there are good guys and bad guys. The good guys may wear a superhero uniform or a white cowboy hat while the bad guys have the black cowboy hats, masks, or some other devious uniform. When good and bad guys exist, one person wins and the other person loses. Someone protects and someone pays, justice and injustice, tipping and balancing repeatedly. "Victim," first used in the 15th century, describes someone who is injured, destroyed, sacrificed, or subject to oppression, hardship, or mistreatment. At some point, you have worn both the white and the black hats by being a victim and an aggressor as you tried to meet your needs with the resources available to you. While "good and bad" and "right and wrong,,"" may look and sound absolute, this is one area that holds many shades of gray.

Bad behavior is the language of the deeply wounded. Most people are much more in touch with their shadow than light qualities. I hear this described as being broken. Some people strive to keep these shadow qualities buried, or at least at bay, while others revel in the darkest crevices of their shadows. Out of balance, in either direction, the shadow side becomes controlling. These shadow emotions can be a form of protection from the pain of your needs not being met or a signal that something dear to you is being threatened. Without balance, you begin the internal cycle of destruction through thoughts and actions, or externally through abusive or aggressive behavior towards others. You disconnect a part of yourself by trying to repress a shadow quality.

Creating and telling the stories of your pain in an attempt to make sense of and elevate the pain is easy. Validation from the sympathy received allows you to feel good, worthy, strong, right, and in control. For the most part, people want to see those they care about be happy, healthy, and safe. When they hear stories of your pain, they do what they can to comfort you. Comfort feels good, especially when you are hurting and it is easier to seek comfort outside of you than from inside.

At some point, you may begin to believe your pain makes you special, that it entitles you in some way, perhaps to simply not have to do the hard work of healing or, worse, ever have to step into your unique expression of the energy of Love. Perhaps you begin to truly believe that this pain is the heavy price of dues that earns you wisdom, honor and privilege. Deep down, though, you know that this isn't true. You tell another story to whomever you can find sympathy from- probably someone who has pain just like yours. Misery does love company, yes?

The way you see the world is a mirror reflecting how you see yourself. When you judge others harshly, it is a reflection what you judge within yourself. That "idiot" you yelled at for driving too slowly, aggressively, or not paying attention? That is you, at least at times. The manager who "doesn't care about anyone other than herself" is you at times. The lover who doesn't understand, is you at times. The shadow emotions that arise are the same intolerance you have for the soft spots within yourself: your need for patience, understanding, acceptance, love, compassion, empathy, mercy, and intimacy. You are called to love others even when you feel they are not worthy. You are called to love yourself even when you feel you are not worthy. That love is what makes them -- and you -- worthy.

Those reflections and the raw spots you feel when your core needs are not being met are your opportunities to heal. Many people are not aware of their wounds. You are, however, aware of your secondary reaction to having those places touched. Some people call them hot buttons. Because these places are calling for healing, they are the places the people you love most are drawn to touch. Not so different than when a child with chicken pox or mosquito bites can't help but scratch, even when repeatedly instructed, "Don't scratch!" The immediate emotion exhibited when the spots are touched is irritability, yet underneath lies sadness, shame, and fear. Breaking the circuit of the initial reaction and then soothing the unhealed wounds gives you an opportunity to finally provide the attention needed for healing. You use your hot buttons as teachers, the emotions as guides, and little by little, with each experience, you begin to re-member and connect those disconnected parts. This seems hard to do in a society that teaches "an eye for an eye." It is easier to be a victim, casting the blame and responsibility on others.

We have all experienced being a victim, though we judge the people who get comfortable playing the victim role. Playing a victim is one way to meet your needs for love, support, acceptance, and affection. Our society is filled with passive-aggressive victims. Choosing, even unconsciously, to be a victim is an inefficient and often costly way to meet your needs. When you feel those unhealed wounds being touched, poked, or prodded, you immediately feel an emotional trigger. These can be subtle triggers, such as a look or a tone of voice. An alarm sounds in your mind, telling you that something bad is coming, and the fight/flight/freeze/submit mode is engaged. You get stuck in patterns when your deepest needs remain unmet. The brain starts trying to figure out what it all means: anger tells you to fight, shame causes you to flee, fear freezes you and despair makes you submit. These patterns become second nature and eventually you don't even notice them. You build stories on "always" and "never," perpetuating the cycles further. For example, after a relationship ends and you say, "I will never let myself get close enough to hurt like that again." Or you say, "I'll always be alone." Both tell your mind to map potential relationships as something to fight and flee.

Shame is a painful feeling arising from the awareness of doing something wrong or having it done to you. Shame can bring disgrace, which is defined as a loss of respect, honor, and esteem. Shame causes a feeling of being wrong, defective, not good enough, inadequate, or not strong enough. The actual sensation of shame is most often felt as "I'm not deserving."

Shame can be expressed through various emotions:
> Shyness is shame in the presence of a stranger, drawn from an underlying belief of not being good enough.
> Discouragement is shame about temporary defeat; where your worth is in question based on the unmet expectations of success.
> Embarrassment is the shame of not feeling adequate or "good enough" in front of others.
> Inferiority is shame about self; the need to play small as a way to gain acceptance or avoid judgment.

Expectations, blocked hopes, disappointment, perceived failure, or any event that weakens a bond in a relationship (including the relationship to self) can trigger shame. At your essence, your core, you are the energy of Love. How can you be anything less than enough? You are perfectly imperfect, beautifully unique. You have skills, gifts, and talents that are necessary to this life. Not one person is like you. You are here in this time and space because you are needed. Anyone who has told you differently was likely projecting his or her own inadequate feelings. Remember, hurt people hurt.

As shyness manifests, know that every single one of us feels inadequate in some way. However, we are all human. We all have to eat and drink to survive. So we all go to the bathroom, our bodies make funny noises, and we all smell funny from time to time. We all have the same emotions and at the core, just about everyone wants the same things. You have something to offer them that is priceless: unconditional love and acceptance. Pretty powerful stuff. As you feel yourself experience shyness, breathe into your belly and know that what you are feeling is nothing more than energy, so encourage that feeling to grow. As you try to increase the energy, you will feel a shift from fear to courage. Then, just be you- perfectly imperfect- sending out love, gratitude, and acceptance to the person you felt shy with and just watch the shift happen. You'll be putting yourself on an even playing field. The more you practice this, the easier it gets. Soon, shyness will rarely, if ever, be an issue for you.

Discouragement is only *temporary* defeat. It is easy to want to attach to the emotion. Keep moving forward. Perhaps it wasn't the right time or quite the right way and the loss is an opportunity for you to reassess and realign. Sit with discouragement and ask your highest self what you need to feel to bring you more courage, hope, and strength in that moment. Using Remembrance, ask what insight the Divine and your guides (energetic entities such as angels) have for you around this situation and listen. Reflect on previous successes and times you overcame adversity. You likely learned valuable lessons through those, so apply them to your present situation. Maintain focus on your desired goal, open your heart to receiving what you need to reach that goal, imagine how it would feel to achieve the goal and grow *that* feeling in you. When you do this, discouragement has no room to exist.

Were you ridiculed or belittled as a child? As an adult, you have the power to change and evolve. You also have the power to embrace and love that part of you that was ridiculed because it is one of your unique gifts, it is what makes you special, so love it! Were you raised to believe that your worth was tied to achievement, compliance, or productivity? Your worth has nothing to do with your income, status, material possessions, how much you do or how well behaved you are. Well behaved people rarely change the world. When you choose to not follow your heart or use your

Divine gifts, your soul is going to nag at you. Even if you achieve great status and vast wealth, something in you will feel off and you will continually self-sabotage. An on-going sense of shame for what you have, lost, and desire keep you stuck until you make a choice to be authentic. Were you raised in a family where blame, finger pointing, or a mentality of being better than others was the norm? When you don't feel good enough or worthy, the ego will use these tactics to make you feel better. The big problem with this mentality is that we are *all* infinite Divine beings with infinite Divine energy. No one's essence is better than another's. Perfectionism is another attempt to mask shame.

When shame appears, sit with it, breathe into it and practice compassion, connection, and courage. Seek ways to increase these qualities in your life right away. Then take action. It's not enough to think about them. If shame is alive because you have done something to meet your needs in a way that has hurt you or someone else, practice and seek forgiveness. We will go deeper into this is chapter 11. Use the experience to see what resources you need to make a better choice in the future.

Guilt is not an emotion; it is a perceived fact or state of having committed an offense, crime, violation, or wrong. Guilt is a judgment. At your core, you have needs. Sometimes you can meet them in a way that is effective, efficient, and least costly. At other times you meet them with the resources available to you, creating shadow emotions in yourself or others. Placing a label of right or wrong only creates a punitive judgment where there is no room to explore better ways to meet those needs. How can you ever learn to meet those needs in the most effective and efficient way possible? How can anyone learn? We are our harshest judge and jury when it comes to deciding guilt and punishment. In dealing with wrongs, crime, and violation, everyone must be able to tell their stories fully and honestly. Try to understand the intentions behind the actions, the consequences of those actions, and determine what can be done to heal the pain. This is how we break the cycles of violence.

"Depression" follows a period of being inauthentic or ignoring emotions and intuition. Because the soul's desires have been ignored, stagnation takes effect. It is as if you want to do something and just don't know how to move forward or you feel as if you can't. Coming out of depression requires you to learn who you are *now*, identify what you feel and what you need. You are ever-changing and evolving. This is an exciting process of learning that makes life a great adventure. Knowing what you believe, value, need, and desire are critical to living authentically. Some of those will remain solid and unwavering, while the rest will evolve. Stepping out of depression requires you to risk taking ownership of your life and releasing the victim role by learning about yourself. As you take one small step in the direction of authenticity, each subsequent step will be much easier and the depression begins to dissolve.

Sadness comes from holding on to a person or situation that has run its course in your life. Yes, it is very painful when you lose someone you love to death or a relationship ends. It is perfectly normal to be sad with such loss. Sadness that lingers after a lesser traumatic experience can dramatically affect you and those in your life. Just as you are ever evolving, so are others. When you try to keep things as they were when you first encountered them, when you lose what you determined was the person you adored, the perfect job, or dream house, the feeling of loss feels much deeper. Overcoming sadness requires you to let go of your grip on the past in order to reinvent and rejuvenate. This also circles back to authenticity. If you had your routine changed for you, ask yourself, "Who do I want be now? Who am I now?" You can never get back the past, so longing for it only holds you prisoner in a prison with no walls and certainly no lock on the gate.

Fear, worry, and anxiety are the emotions around the fear of judgment. Everyone has a deep need for acceptance, belonging, and love. There is a risk associated with stepping into your authenticity because there will be some loss. Some people who have been in your life will no longer have a place when you begin to be true to yourself. You could lose your sense of security or financial stability if your authenticity leads you away from an ill-suited job. Fear, worry, and anxiety are limiting and they will paralyze your decision making abilities. This takes you into the flight or freeze mode. You simply have to choose an action towards your authenticity. There are no right or wrong decisions. There is only the choice of meeting your needs in the most effective, efficient, and least costly way. Even if your choice takes you off the path your soul longs to travel, eventually you will return. Every side journey is an opportunity to gain experiences and wisdom. Focus on your breath. Listen to your heart and pay attention to your body. If you feel constricted, you are not being authentic. If you feel open, spacious, and light, you are in your space of authentic truth. Obviously in the case of anxiety disorders and phobias, deeper work needs to occur in the healing process. Please seek professional help when you need it.

Being suicidal is the disconnection between being your authentic self and the false identity you have created. YOU do not need to die! The false identity, the lies, the sense of unworthiness, and lovelessness *do* need to die. I was lying on my back next to one of my closest friends, staring up at the stars in Mexico, listening to the waves crash on the shore. All I could think of was, "Why am I still here?" I was not depressed. In fact, I felt fairly at peace. I simply did not see a purpose to my life. I walked into the waves a few days later with no intent of coming out. I was completely disconnected from my authentic self. I was evolving, but at a pace I could not recognize because it was so slow. While my actions were suicidal, my emotions were in a state of despair. I was pulled out of those waves. A few days later, I met my authentic self. It took killing the false identity to create enough space to let the real me be present. I do not, under any circumstances, recommend trying this in a similar manner. I was lucky that day that someone was there and had the skills necessary to help me. "Killing" the false self often requires some external wisdom to transition from who you've been to your authentic self. It can also be done through a ritual, similar to many indigenous initiation ceremonies. Do not be afraid to ask for help. The National Suicide Prevention Hotline is 1-800-273-8255.

Despair is an emotion that evolves from the deep disconnection from your essence. It can either bring about destruction or the ultimate in creation. When you reach despair, you turn your back on help from everyone in order to fully absorb the toxicity of the experience. At some point the soul's survival mechanism kicks in, dropping you to your knees causing you to plea for help. This is extreme self-love. The soul reminds you, "You ain't done yet, kid." Getting face-to-face with your pain, or unmet needs, and being willing to take responsibility for your part provides the space to begin healing. By doing so, you are able to return to your path and create the life you chose in your sacred contract. Remaining a victim, blaming others, and giving away your power will destroy your faith, integrity, relationships, and joy for living.

Anger creates a primary urge to attack. In response, the body often tenses through the neck and jaw trying to repress the urge. Anger is about feeling shortchanged, rejected, hurt physiologically or emotionally. It can stem from an interference with a desire, or an injustice. This emotion controls, punishes, and retaliates. Anger feeds on anger and multiplies. If a person can become aware of their anger rather than express it, they can pause momentarily to try to separate from that spiral. Anger is useful in telling you when your boundaries have been threatened. Trying to repress anger keeps your boundaries unprotected. Expressing anger at every threat also leaves those boundaries exposed. As you feel the anger arise, ask yourself what boundary is being threatened? Use the breath to give yourself time to shift from the primal part of the brain that acts on autopilot in the fight or flee mode into the more rational part of the brain. Consider how to stand your ground, communicate your feelings and needs, and make a request or reasonable demand. We will cover this process in more detail in chapter 13. One additional thing you can do to calm the anger if it continues to increase, is to relax your hands, then the shoulders, and finally the jaw while breathing slowly and deeply. Anger is not a bad emotion, just an easily out-of-control emotion. Understanding how to use it effectively and efficiently is a powerful skill. With help, you can learn to become aware of your anger allowing yourself to meet your needs before reaching a state of rage.

Rage is the biological urge to kill. When experienced, the frontal brain shuts down, making it impossible to step back and observe the emotions. The emotions take over completely. If you are experiencing rage, please seek professional guidance. Somatic experiencing is an effective means of physically releasing the energy. Rage is a reaction to hurt. Neither good nor bad, how you react to it can make all the difference in healing or remaining stuck in an ever-widening downward spiral of pain and destruction.

Awareness of your emotions allows you to better control your impulses to react to situations. It is the circuit breaker of your internal wiring. Emotions are your guides and quite possibly your most valuable tools to living authentically. You can redirect from an inefficient or ineffective means of meeting your needs to a more appropriate way. Even a fraction of a second of awareness can make all the difference in deconstructing the developing story, to evaluate if this is true or not, real or not. This allows you to see the multitude of options available rather than the same old destructive patterns of hurt that you may be used to. It takes effort to master, just as any skill does. However, you can start practicing right now. How are you feeling? So what? Now what?

When you try to repress feeling anger, hatred, sadness, or fear, you cut off a part of you. What is the longing below the shadow? Can you invite the shadow in, love it, and learn from it? By integrating the shadow and light qualities into a place of balance, the shadows begin to guide you and serve as a measuring post. They provide a space to view others more empathetically and compassionately. Ultimately you are able to accept the shadow within other people, becoming more compassionate, loving, and forgiving.

Transitioning from being a victim of your pain to surviving and finally to thriving starts by taking 100% responsibility for your acts, even the most trivial acts. There are no coincidences and there are no accidents. When you accept responsibility for your life, your choices, your thoughts, and your emotions, and release the blame, you gain power. Accepting responsibility is bitter at first. With time though, it becomes sweeter and stronger. Your past may define you presently. However, it certainly does not have to define your future. Start looking now at your own feelings and allow the armor of false identity and limiting beliefs to start falling away. Take responsibility for your beliefs. This is all you, my friend. Looking to others for all the answers is fruitless. You have the answers within you. You always have.

Surviving

Being a survivor is complicated. Surviving is a type of instinct. You are still here. The question is what/who did not survive? Perhaps it was a piece of you, your dream, a relationship, an important person in your life, a job, or a home. It could be any number of things. There is a level of guilt around that knowledge. Sure, you survived, but at what cost? You need to grieve and mourn the loss. Grief is the personal, internal response to loss. How you respond to your loss will be unique to you, your resources (internal and external), and your support network (or lack of). Loss brings up many emotions and questions. Why did this happen? What did I do (or not do)? Loss and grief tap the deepest, darkest spots, activating vulnerability.

When loss is experienced, you need to feel safe in order to fully grieve. If someone is telling you to suck it up, don't worry about it, or get over it, the message is that it is not ok to grieve. You may need time to yourself. Going into nature can be helpful, even if that is as simple as just going for a walk. Breathing the fresh air helps to clear the mind and the body of cortisol which is a hormone secreted in times of high stress. You need space to reflect and remember, explore what the loss means, its purpose, and what is next. Such insight brings acceptance of the loss and that is a necessary step that helps you integrate the loss into your identity.

As grief arises, know that these emotions are okay. There is room for all emotions: speculation, anger, feeling lost, abandoned, afraid, alone, impatient, intolerant, judgmental, jealous, resentment, envy, pride, and even cruelty. These emotions are the ego's way of trying to protect you from the pain of the loss. Feel them in that moment and be willing to let them go because in your heart, you know the emotions are not you. You are the energy of Love and as such, you are not alone. You are connected to the whole of the world. All you have to do is reach out and ask for support, love, mercy, tenderness. Notice what your heart desires and ask the Divine to fill your heart. You have everything you need within you or your reach..

Ultimately, as you process your grief, you are seeking ways to live harmoniously. You learn to balance shadow and light, pain and joy. Both do co-exist. Write out your grief to get it out of your head. You can put it in water and freeze it or burn the pages if you choose. Take the emotions swirling inside of you and remove them from your body. Just like with children, darkness engages the imagination and monsters become scary things. However, once the light is on, there is nothing there. Writing helps to shine the light on the scary emotions. Left to swirl internally, those emotions can feel bigger and harder than you believe you have the strength to face and feel. When written or spoken aloud, they appear quite normal. They lose their power.

Grieving is not an easy process. Sometimes it can be overwhelming. That is why there are professionals who are experts in trauma healing. Sometimes, the lack of grieving can create patterns that impact one or more areas of your life. Processing the loss can eliminate those patterns.

You survived because your instinct guided you. In the battles of life you somehow subconsciously attempted to prove that you are good, loving, kind, and capable, you fought the good fight. It was not the relationship, the job, or the goal so much as it was your sense of worth that you fought so hard to feel. People place a tremendous weight on external factors for validation. Though you may feel like it, you have never had to prove your worth. You always *have been* and *always will be* the energy of Love, which carries its own strength, greatness, and compassion. Every time you feel the need to prove that you are right, strong, in control, provider and protector, it is a battle that you cannot win. You are fighting yourself for something that already exists within you.

Here you are, survivor. You can choose to set up the armor to protect you from feeling that pain again or you can transform it. Transforming requires you to get downright messy, face your shadow emotions, identify your needs, and learn how to meet them. As you do this, you begin to create space to help others do the same. Surrender yourself right now. Just rest back into the faith that you are supported. You don't have to figure out anything. You don't have to fix anything. You just have to be you. Celebrate the survival! Mourn the losses. Take time to let go of your attachment to the stories. You'll know when it is time to pick it up and resume the journey. There is a point between surviving and thriving in which day-to-day living can feel too arduous to survive. You will. You may feel horribly vulnerable. That doesn't make you weak. It makes you real.

Being vulnerable is different from being a victim. In vulnerability, you are capable of being physically or emotionally wounded without hiding, avoiding, or staying stuck. It is real. It hurts. It sucks. It takes courage to go there, admit it, ask for help if needed, and do the work to heal the hurt. Few have that strength. For those who do, they leap into the faith of the unknown and find grace arming them with their most valuable tool, Love.

Moving from surviving to thriving is about being willing to own up to your parts in life. It is about being willing to touch the raw spots and see what is needed to heal. It is about being willing to feel. Being willing does not make it happen. It takes work. The good news is that you're a survivor. Now, you have to learn to use your feelings as the trusted guides they were always meant to be rather than ignoring or repressing them.

You have been on a passage of rites, an initiation of sorts. You were sent out to overcome a challenge and find your inner strength, courage, and intuition. When you experience a life changing event, heartbreak, or death, you are broken down and built back up in a way that creates a new wisdom and view on the world. These experiences *shape* you. In the long journey home from this experience, who is there to welcome you into the circle of transformation? You return changed, but you can't quite explain how or why. This transformation begins to separate you from the people you once felt close to. The disconnection makes the soul search for a way to make sense of it all. Maybe you retreat internally or maybe you seek another opportunity to experience something to transform the pain. Now it is time to learn what you need and how to communicate those needs.

Needs

This chapter contains many questions. They are springboards to
help you dive deeper into what you need and why. You may find
even more questions bubbling to the surface as you explore. To
help with such a deep level of introspection, I like to use a practice
from the Sufi religion called The Remembrance. This is a practice
of reverence in which you actively engage the Divine (God, Source,
Great Spirit- whatever name you use) in a relationship. You are
seeking guidance and providing quiet space to listen to the wisdom
of the Divine, your guides, angels, archangels, or ancestors. You
can ask them to show you the Truth, for support, or guidance. If
you do not believe in a higher source, simply ask the wisdom of
evolution, nature, and space to provide perspective for you.

Remembrance begins by calling out to the Divine to join you in
your heart. Growing up, I lived across the street from a park. When
it was time to go home in the evening, my parents would flash the
front porch light. If I did not see it (or ignored it), they would open
the door and start calling my name. The whole neighborhood
could hear them! This is how I envision calling the Divine. I also
imagine inviting in the Divine as I would a friend to join me for tea
and a talk. Use whatever image works best for you. With each
breath, you call the name of the Divine, by whatever name you
normally use in prayer, if you pray. If you do not, you can still use
this practice, imagining falling into the vastness of space. Pause and
notice how your body feels before you call out again. I notice the
presence of the Divine by a sense of calm flowing through my
body.

Take the painful or shadowy feeling you discover during the needs
exploration and place it in front of the Divine. Ask what would

51

harmonize this feeling? Be willing to risk being surprised by the response. Your mind will bring up what you *think* you need. You will know it is your mind because it won't ring true throughout your body. Soul answers are quick and simple, without any stories or rationalizations. Just listen. You may perceive one or more qualities that are unfamiliar such as: mercy, reverence, equanimity. If the qualities are unfamiliar, ask to be shown how the qualities feel and what they would look like in your life. Ask to have your heart filled with the quality. If you have never felt it, imagine what it would feel like. Then, just allow yourself to feel.

When you feel full, extend gratitude for whatever insights you just received. In this way, you are using observation, awareness, and harmony to bring balance and healing, rather than judgment and the urge to "fix." There is nothing broken. Making yourself wrong through the judgment of feelings only takes you deeper into the stuck space. As you harmonize the feelings back into the energy of Love, you springboard out of the stuck space. Now, let's explore needs.

The connotation of being needy is negative, which is ironic because every single person has needs that started before they were born. You needed the sperm and egg to fertilize in order for your existence to begin. You needed your mother's body, blood, nourishment, and protection to gestate until it was time for you to come into this world for your first breath. You needed someone to feed you, protect you, change your diapers, bathe, and shelter you until you were able to take over those responsibilities. Your needs did not end there, though.

I never knew how profound the question, "What do you need?" was until I began to explore why I did what I did, thought what I thought, and felt what I felt during my healing process. An unmet need is likely what caused a break in the flow of Love energy. The discomfort or pain from that break brought questions, then thoughts and stories, followed by beliefs. Those beliefs can rationalize away the ability to meet future needs. I did not know what *I* needed. Many of my clients do not know what *they* need. One client expressed this best by sharing, "I don't have the language to express my needs." In order to communicate needs, you first must be able to identify them.

Abraham Maslow identified a hierarchy of needs in his 1954 book *Motivation and Personality* as physiological, belongingness and love, esteem, self-actualization, and self-transcendence. Though these needs are structured in a hierarchy, humans move up and down the hierarchy all the time. Maslow theorized that humans are motivated by these needs, and their successful development is based on meeting them. Without the basic fundamental needs first being met however, none of the others can be fully realized.

The need for survival is hardwired into each of us. If your basic needs are unmet, you will have difficulty focusing on much else. Unfortunately, even the perception that the basic physiological needs are unmet can slow or even halt the ability to focus on the other four higher categories.   As we explore these needs, ask yourself if your unmet needs are real or a perception? Creating *perceived* unmet needs is a subconscious trick to help you heal an old wound. If you are creating such needs, ask yourself, "What am I trying to heal?" Ask yourself if you are ready to heal. It is okay if you are not. You will be ready when you are ready and you will know when that time arrives.

A counselor told me once that the age when a person experienced their first significantly life-altering event will be the age they emotionally revert in times of stress and pain. I return to being four years old. If you have ever witnessed a four year old having a meltdown, they are irrational and difficult to negotiate with until they calm down. If you're not the person who occasioned or is experiencing that meltdown, there's a fascination to witnessing that behavior in unhappy adults. Their actions, even their facial expressions will reflect, if ever so slightly, the pouty six year old, the petulant nine year old, the defiant teenager. Sometimes the affect can be heard in the tone of voice.

Typically, there will be one or two particular needs that inner child demands. Take a moment to reflect back to times you have felt angry or hurt. How did you feel? How did you react? Can you perceive yourself reacting emotionally or internally as a child would have? I would encourage you to invite that hurt child to join you for this process of discovering needs. He or she will be an excellent guide. Imagine talking to him/her in your mind's eye. Most of the time, your child just needs to feel safe enough to dream, believe, express, grow, and be loved and accepted. How can you facilitate that? Imagine if you could have had the desired security, love and acceptance as a child, how would that have felt? How would it have looked and sounded? Often, I encourage my clients to play like they did at that age. They are always amazed at the breakthroughs and epiphanies that occur when they allow themselves to play again.

One of the most basic needs is security. Insecurity is a common theme not only with my clients, but also as a collective with our society. The fear of not feeling secure ranges from subtle to paralyzing. On a subtle level, it manifests as having to work harder, make more money, and accumulate more material possessions. For others, the focus is the "lack of" and the inability to fill that void. Lack leads to a scarcity mentality that impacts the way you define success and the methods by which you strive for success. Although you may have the security of a safe, temperate place to sleep and contain your possessions, in your mind your need for security is not being met.

What makes you feel safe and secure? This could be shelter and employment. It is often more. I remember living in a historic downtown neighborhood in a large city. Many homeless people wandered my neighborhood while drug trafficking and gang activity operated all around. Many of my neighbors' homes were broken into. Yet, even as a single woman living alone, I felt safe enough to sleep with my windows open in comfortable weather. My friends who come from a completely different mindset were quick to tell me all the reasons why I needed a weapon to protect myself in such a neighborhood. Everyone has different standards of safety and security, each with a unique reason why.

What were your beliefs around security as a child? Your parents might have shown their fear about money and providing for the family or they might have demonstrated the fear of not having enough love and attention. What about now? What do you need to feel secure? Is security associated with money. While money can provide shelter, food, and clothing, you really do not need much money to provide those. In many places in the world, people survive on less than a dollar a day. Or is security based on love and attention? If so, how much is enough? Spend some time with this question of what makes you feel secure and why.

Stability and consistency are as important emotionally as they are physically. Families that move frequently, such as those in the military, do not have an opportunity to really participate in community or create strong bonds of friendship. After a while, their children stop trying to assimilate or make friends: a habitual emotional distance that follows them into adult relationships. As adults living a nomadic life may feel more familiar. How do you create physical stability and consistency? Do you follow a routine or fly by the seat of your pants? Do you have roots and emotional investments in your community? Humans are tribal. In our global society, these tribes are no longer traditional, but are broken into different geographic locations. Nearby families and long-term neighbors who used to provide a support network no longer exist. You have to develop your own tribe. We need that tribe to feel safe enough; to be vulnerable and to receive love, acceptance, and wisdom. We also need to share those gifts with others in their time of need. Otherwise, you simply feel isolated and alone. That is a sure way to remaining stuck.

We are wired to be a part of a tribe and having a sense of belonging is extremely important. If you are more introverted, this is a challenging task. Children who had attentive caretakers likely grew up to be adults who met their own needs to belong and love. Without that early attachment, as adults, you will bring to your life people and situations to try to heal these unmet needs. Think of how you seek acceptance and belonging. What does community mean to you? Have you ever felt accepted or that you belonged? Have you ever felt like an integral part of a community? Do you feel you matter? Have you ever felt you did not matter?

Living in an environment with emotional instability and inconsistency can produce strong survival skills impacting the ability to trust. Being hyper-vigilant causes a person to constantly be in the fight or flight mode, which equally affects both physiology and psychology. Ironically, as an adult you may attract wounded people as an attempt to heal this need for emotional stability and consistency. Or you may place yourself in situations where it is difficult to hold a job because you have a deep need to be cared for and supported. Take an honest look at where you are at in your life and who else is with you. What needs are you trying to meet through these relationships and situations? Expecting your needs to be met by others is a heavy burden for that 'someone else' to carry. Usually they won't even know your needs because you haven't expressed them. So when they fail to meet your expectations, they are understandably confused when you are hurt and upset. Who in your life provides emotional consistency and stability? How do you provide that for yourself? Being honest with yourself about stability is a challenge. Quite honestly, taking ownership initially sucks because you realize how much you are responsible for where you are right now. However, if you stay committed to building on your current successes in this area, you will discover the ultimate empowerment and liberation.

Support is both a physical and emotional need. Many people I know were raised in an environment where support was minimal. The mindset of, "Your problems are yours, deal with them and don't expect others to help you" becomes an engrained belief. While masked as the need to be strong and independent, this need is rooted in distrust and fear of vulnerability. Such mentality is counter to most world cultures where supporting one another is the norm, particularly within families and villages. Even the hardest shell can be cracked by love. The crack can be caused by nature, animals, and sometimes humans. The essence will persist, even when it is resisted thoroughly. "I'm fine. I don't need help!" can only last for so long before the body manifests the density as pain or disease or someone or something appears to crack the shell.

Did you feel physically and emotionally supported as a child? If not, what would you have needed to feel supported? How do you feel supported now? If you struggle to answer that, how would you *imagine* it feels to be supported? How do you support yourself? Is your body trying to get you to support yourself by manifesting pain or disease?

The flip side of not reaching out for needed support is a sense of entitlement, or expecting others to support you. This could be a learned behavior or a deeply subconscious response to an unmet childhood need. If you lacked support growing up, you may desire someone else care for you physically or emotionally as an adult. You may give your power away, refuse to take responsibility or blame others for your situation in order to receive support. You allow yourself to become a victim in order to meet your needs. Taking ownership of your feelings and needs is scary. I know. Yet staying a victim sucks. If it worked you wouldn't have picked up this book. It's time to step up and do something about it. Now. Even if all you do is say, "I'm surrendering being a victim."

As an infant, you learn to trust when your needs are met. Trust is broken when you discover information provided to you was intentionally incorrect, even if this was not done maliciously. Trust is fragile and requires much work to re-establish once broken. Sometimes it cannot be re-established with others. How do you trust? How do you earn trust? How do you trust yourself? Having your natural skills and talents repressed also impacts your ability to trust; you no longer feel safe enough to be authentic. You protect yourself from fear (of failure, success, and people) by judging others and yourself. That judgment disconnects you from the energy of Love and creates distrust. People cannot read your mind or your heart to know what you need. If you don't share, they cannot know.

Not being able to communicate needs and feelings leads to self-*mis*trust because you give away your power by relying on others to make you feel something or meet your needs. All of these can play a role in your confidence in others and yourself. Do you have difficulty trusting others? What or who broke your trust as a child? Teen? Young adult? Do you trust yourself? What would it take for you to trust yourself? In what ways do you allow others or material possessions to set the value of your self-worth? Trust requires risk. Are you willing to risk seeing that the people around you have insecurities, fears, joys, hopes and dreams much like you? Are you willing to risk seeing beyond their actions into their essence as you explore what you need and how their actions or words may have failed to meet those needs?

The more open you are to following your instinct, the more you can trust yourself. If you ignore your instinct,-you will find yourself repeatedly in situations that challenge your trust in yourself or others. Having your natural skills and talents repressed also impacts your ability to trust; you no longer feel safe enough to be authentic. Self-trust can exist when you get reacquainted with your feelings and needs, are willing to feel everything, and can use feelings as guides to keep your life on track. Self-trust begins with each small step you take toward authenticity.

Physical wellbeing seems like an obvious need to meet, yet the past two decades of my career have been filled with people who have failed to meet this need. Physical well-being is about having enough food, air, water, rest, physical activity, and sexual expression to *optimally* live, not merely survive. There is a big difference between having enough sufficient calories to exist physically and having nutrient-dense foods that provides not just cellular support but also energy. There is a difference between fresh, clean water and water that has been recycled, first through people, then through municipal systems that cannot filter out all of the chemicals, pharmaceuticals, or toxins. There is a difference between walking through the woods and walking down the street in a major metropolitan area. There is a difference between sleeping fitfully and being well rested. Being physically active increases your energy level while decreasing your stress level. "Getting off" is much different than being fully engaged in your sexuality and connecting on a deep (no pun intended) level. Notice how your energy feels when you engage in various activities, minimizing activities that drain your energy and maximizing activities that increase your energy.

Physical well-being needs can serve as medication or ignored entirely. Do you choose foods that provide nutrients that your body needs to run optimally or are you feeding something other than physical hunger when you eat? What beneficial physical activity do you enjoy? How often do you engage in it? How much water do you drink? Do you spend some time daily consciously focusing on your breath, both deepening and slowing it? Do you get enough rest, and of what quality? How do you express yourself sexually? What hangups and judgments do you have about sex?

Physical well-being is truly about balance. You may need to have someone teach you how to exercise in a way that is both fun and safe. You may need to learn both what foods will optimally fuel you and how to prepare them. Listening to your body can give you the biggest clues to tell if these basic needs are being met. Your energy level, weight and skin will reflect your level of balance. Take small steps in the direction of balance. Celebrate and build on your successes and balance will become second nature.

Taking care of self is a demonstration of self-love. You are showing affection for yourself. The Dalai Lama says, "Affection is important because it counters anger, hatred and suspicion that can prevent our minds from functioning clearly." How do you seek affection? How do you show affection? I encourage my clients to give when they most need to receive affection. If you were to pick up the phone and call a friend and say, "Hey, I was just thinking about you and how much you mean to me. I just wanted you to know." You will undoubtedly get a little love back which for most of us is easier than calling and saying, "I need to feel loved right now. Can you share some love?" Actually, both of these scenarios work.

When you touch and hug, your body produces oxytocin, the bonding hormone that makes you feel closer to someone, and that also reduces blood pressure. For many people hugs bring up the unworthiness and sense of shame, instigating a pat on the back. My dear friend, Joshua, taught me how to be hugged. It was one of the most precious gifts I have ever received. When he hugs, he puts his whole heart in it. It is a body to body contact and there's none of this patting the back stuff. When you are hugged by Joshua, you *know* that you are worthy of and are being loved unconditionally. What role does intimacy play in your life? Are you able to engage intimacy outside of sexual expression? If you are craving the sense of touch, start with allowing yourself to be touched. Manicures, pedicures, and massages are a great way to experience being touched. Then, start practicing with a light, compassionate, friendly touch on a friend's arm when you're making a point. Allow yourself to hug and be hugged. Incorporate intimacy slowly and build upon each success.

How do you show appreciation? These are the kind gestures you do for others to make life a little more enjoyable. Though you may *know* you appreciate the people in your life, unless you show it, they may not know. Actions speak louder than words. How do you like to be shown that you are appreciated? How do you communicate your feelings, particularly when they have been hurt? Do you feel compassion towards others or are you judgmental? Are you able to show yourself compassion?

Respect is something everyone desires, and yet, it can be completely ambiguous. Respect has to do with consideration and holding a person in esteem or honoring their worth and value. You want respect because you want your worthiness validated. Respect is very much give-and-take. The person you most need to respect is yourself because you teach people how to treat you by your actions. If you do not take care of yourself, you are subliminally teaching others you are not worthy of their respect because you are not worthy of your *own* respect. What does respect mean to you? How do you show respect? How do you desire to be respected? Is there a difference in what you want and what you actually do in regards to respect?

When you feel you are being disrespected, you are experiencing a guided moment to look at your own integrity, self-worth, and sense of value. How do you compromise your integrity? Telling yourself you will lose weight and eat healthy, for example, and then choosing foods that are unhealthy is breaking integrity with yourself. Not keeping promises. Allowing yourself to be taken advantage of because you don't feel right to speak up about your worth will create a disrespecting scenario. You believe you are not valuable, you teach others to treat you as such, which ultimately feels disrespectful.

Respect can be increased by:
- actively listening to others without trying to one-up or prove your worthiness by sharing your story
- treating yourself and others with dignity, courtesy, and compassion at all times
- commit to integrity- keep your word, commitments, and promises
- be patient with yourself and others
- be able to back your opinions with facts or keep them to yourself
- engage sincerity, generosity, and humility in your life
- honor others as Divine, infinite beings.

Self-esteem and self-actualization are what we are working toward in this book. Becoming authentic. Who are you now? Who do you want to be? What makes you tick? Awareness and consciousness elevate as you begin to process how you feel and what you need. Communicate and seek to meet your needs in the most effective, efficient way possible. You will become more creative in your thinking, storytelling, and problem solving skills. How do you currently express your creativity? How open are you to discovery? Do you live from a place of integrity? What are your values? Do you stand by those values or do you compromise to meet other needs?

As you become more adept at meeting your needs, you can move into self-transcendence. This is knowing that you *do* play a role in this life and in some way, everyone is connected. You have unique gifts and are here in this world right now for a specific reason. Autonomy is about knowing your authenticity and living it unapologetically. How can you be your own person without losing yourself in relationships, your career, as a parent? What does freedom mean to you? What does independence feel like? Can you ever be fully independent? We all need one another in order to live out our sacred contract and to more fully experience all of the qualities of the Divine. What about independence is most attractive to you? Honor your authenticity. Honor the authenticity of others. Continue to develop your own and respect a sacred space for others to develop their authenticity. Independence and freedom are really about taking responsibility for your feelings, actions and reactions, then practicing unconditional love for yourself and others.

What do you believe in firmly or are passionate about? What are your values and beliefs? If you have no convictions, you can be manipulated through shame or guilt. How do you make choices? Everyone has gut feelings, "red flags" and other subtle warnings when something is wrong. You also know when something is really right. Use that power. Remain committed to listening to your inner wisdom. Seek guidance from the Divine. What does empowerment look and feel like for you? Can you feel safe enough and trust yourself enough to self-express? If not, what would it take to change that?

What is your purpose? If you don't know, try this exercise. Take out a piece of paper and write at the top, "What is my purpose?" Write anything that comes to mind, say "thank you" and ask, "What else?" Repeat until you write the one thing that makes your heart open and you feel like crying. I know it sounds crazy. Just try it. I knew mine when everything I did to get away from my purpose failed and I realized that no matter how hard I tried to walk away, I couldn't because I was continually pulled back. You know there is something that just makes your heart sing or dance, something you are powerfully drawn to and likely scares you a little. Your purpose is simultaneously easy and challenging, which is what makes it exciting enough to keep working toward.

Initially, when you begin the process of identifying feelings and needs, you are so focused on healing that you become hyper-vigilant. Self-judgment arises when you are aware of repeating an old pattern. Stop and sit with what you are feeling, dive deeper, and be willing to risk being surprised at what you may find. As you become more skilled at identifying your thoughts, feelings, and needs, you may judge others for not being awake and aware in their own conscious process. Be compassionate and know that everyone has their own journey, growth, and healing. We all have a choice in how we want to live. Judging someone for his or her choice takes you out of the energy of Love.

There is a sweetness that comes from the hope of freedom from suffering. When you can identify and begin to strive to meet your needs in the most effective and efficient way possible, you develop strength, determination, and empowerment. You find a conviction for living. Why do you do what you do? When you do not know, the offhand comment of how you should or should not do something will pull you away from your confidence and authenticity. In balance, a rhythm exists that flows. Without it, we know something is missing.

Just like an infant learning how to roll, rock, pull, crawl, pull up, teeter, walk, then run, so too you must learn how to live in the body, feel, be aware, and be responsible. When you accept your responsibility in any situation, when you are honest about where the pain is originating from, you can transition from surviving to thriving.

Patterns

Almost everyone has a little box where they store their pain. For some, it's not big and doesn't require much security. For others it is like a matryohka, or Russian doll; a box inside a larger box inside an even larger box. Only this box is then set in concrete, wrapped with an enormous chain, bound with industrial sized padlocks and buried really, really deep. Regardless of how deep you bury your container, your deepest fears and pain will always be *with* you.

Like Superman with X-ray vision, your subconscious sees right through the containers, knows the pain on a cellular level, and does everything it can to harmonize the pain back into the energy of Love. The subconscious brings new people and situations to your life in an attempt to heal the hurt. The ego, on the other hand, wants to protect you from any additional pain and it does everything it can to divert you in a different direction. Most people, however, sense the ego and subconscious's work as an internal war; confusing, frustrating, and never-ending.

Typically, when the brain recognizes a situation as a potentially painful experience, the ego engages raw feelings to warn you of impending disaster. All you know in that moment is to react. Later, when you can renegotiate the meaning of that situation, you can then experience those emotions without being pulled back into the hurt and use them to identify what you really need in that moment. In other words, you deactivate the connection between hot buttons and reaction. You reprogram what had taken your brain into a fight or flight mode. Now when the painful triggers are primed to fire, conflict is less likely to ensue. That is liberation. Without the over-sensitive wiring, you can actually address the facts of the situation dispassionately, effectively, and efficiently. That is empowerment and self-efficacy.

To prepare for this to occur, let's play social scientist. Releasing judgment and proceeding with curiosity, explore and see if you can find patterns in your behavior. What is your epic story of pain? Who has hurt you? If you experienced hurt, whether intentional or not, put it on the list. List them along with the emotional and/or physical pain you experienced and identify the perpetrator. Don't forget to put yourself on that list! You can be both the wrongdoer and the wronged. Take some time to dig into this muck and mire. Get really messy with it because hopefully it is the last time you'll ever need to, unless you choose to repeat these unhappy stories. Don't hold back.

Go through your list and figure out which are the recurring hurts. What are the most significant hurts that have impacted your life? What keeps you from really living authentically? As you identify this, notice where you feel the hurt in your body. Just feel. You may use the list at the back of the book if that helps you identify the feeling(s) more clearly. How do you know that is what you are feeling? What does your body feel like in that place right now? Observe the sensation as if you are a researcher in the field, a participant-observer whose goal is to *learn about* pain rather than *finding* a particular outcome.

What is alive in you? Identify what is even deeper than the sensation you initially described. Go beyond emotions. How would you describe this sensation? Does it have a color? Do you feel it as a throbbing, crushing, dull, achy, heavy, tender, sharp, numb, hot, cold, or suffocating sensation? Identify the pain and ask, "What *is* this?" Sometimes an image would come to mind, sometimes a memory, sometimes a word. I sat with it and *felt* it until it began to loosen its grip. I allowed the pain to use my vocal chords to "speak," creating the most amazing sounds that are sometimes frightening. Then I simply accepted it in that moment for whatever it was and nothing more; no stories or beliefs. I always felt it relax in that moment, bringing relief.

What behaviors stem from this feeling? When I was in pain, my behavior was quite different. I was intolerant, closed-off and destructive. As I accepted the feelings and began to heal, I began to flow with the energy of Love and my creative source resurfaced. When you feel constricted, you are less likely to give or receive. The sensation you are experiencing around the feeling is likely connected to a core belief, one that drives your actions and attracts other people and situations to validate the belief.

You may deeply be longing for someone to comfort you, ease the pain, let you know everything will be all right while the ego strikes up its song and dance of the need to be strong, independent, and in control. Or the heart deeply longs to be taken care of while the ego convinces you that you are not capable or worthy of taking care of yourself, being successful. Or you will be hurt if you take the risk to reach self-efficacy and beyond.

Are these feelings and behaviors ego-based or real? Anger or sadness may be the ego masking the vulnerability of the true feelings - the fear of being abandoned or unworthy. When an emotion is ego driven, it feels heavy and constricted. When it is real, it feels light and expansive. I use the example of a tennis racquet or golf club. Both have sweet spots. When the ball connects to the sweet spot, you feel it through your whole body, and it feels good! When you connect to the edges around the racquet or club, it feels twangy, and you naturally tense a little (or a lot depending how poor the shot was). The same is true for a beautiful song. When a crystal clear note is hit, you feel it flow through your body. When a note is sung off key, you constrict automatically. You simply know how it feels when something feels 'on' or 'off'.

What needs are connected to the feelings? This takes some time to get used to processing. With time, identifying becomes almost second nature. Once you are aware of your patterns, you can differentiate between your ego-driven verses soul-driven actions. You can feel yourself physically bracing and can use your body as well as feelings to get a solid grip on your thoughts and redirect them into a more grounded space. I encourage you to use the Remembrance practice (chapter 4) as you explore.

In certain parts of the world, monkeys were trapped using hollowed coconuts containing some grains of rice left on the trail. The monkey could easily slip a paw inside the coconut. Once it grabbed the grain of rice, the monkey's fist was too large to slip through the opening. Despite the fact that food surrounded the monkey off the trail, the fear of not finding it or the greed of finding this particular meal was too great for the monkey to unclench its fist, let go of the grain, and slip its paw out of the coconut. Your mind is similar to the monkey's fist. You cling to ideas that do not serve you like the monkey clings to the rice. Perhaps you are afraid of not finding what does serve you? You are expressing your Love and playing with others who have chosen to do the same. The immediate payoff of the familiar is greater than what you imagine for the unknown because the familiar meets a need, even if not in the most effective, efficient, least costly way of meeting it.

You cling to the need for love even when what you are receiving is merely attention, positive or negative. You cling to relationships, houses, or jobs far too long, out of comfort, pride, or fear. These are the patterns that need to be broken. You created the story that formed the belief. Now you know how to identify what you are feeling, where you are feeling it, and the need(s) at your core. Create a new story. Sound too easy? Well, it is and it isn't.

Right now, think about everything great in your life. How many things can you think of? Can you come up with five things? What about ten? Twenty five? Fifty? For whatever reason, we are conditioned to focus on the bad stuff, even when life is great. We live in a mental economy of scarcity; there is never enough. We can never be good enough, if only we had (fill in the blank), we'd be happy. These Automatic Negative Thoughts (ANTs) pull us away from the present and reality. They are the rigid ego's resources for reinforcing faulty mental models and beliefs. We allow these thoughts and self-talk to control us.

The clients I work with will either believe that they are "not good enough," a victim, or say they are "fine" when their actions speak otherwise. Beliefs need to be validated in order to remain beliefs. The clients who feel they are not good enough engage in self-sabotaging behavior. The clients who believe they are victims employ a poverty mentality. They give their power away to others by releasing accountability and responsibility for their own actions and choices. The people who say they are fine are simply trying to put on the image of being strong and in control. Meanwhile, internally, they are repressing anger, sadness, and/or fear, and trapping it in their body. They are unable to trust themselves or others. There runs a full gamut of ANTs. Because these thoughts are so automatic, sometimes it is difficult to be aware of the patterns.

To change your pattern, you need to learn how to shift perspective. What you put your attention on is amplified. Energy flows where attention goes. What you resist will persist. Clichés, yet poignant. When something is not working, you want to find and fix the problem at the cost of much attention, energy, and time. The investment of energy magnifies the problem. When you are in financial hardship, for instanced, the awareness of your responsibilities can be a heavy burden, "How am I going to pay my bills?" you wonder. Your focus becomes so fixated on what you do not have, that you cease to remember or recognize your assets. The fear of not having enough can become so large that it feels like it will become a permanent state. Shifting your perspective to identify what is working at the moment opens a wealth of opportunities.

When you are aware of a problem, release the urge to fix it because it is not broken! You may need to heal and meet a need that has gone unmet for a long time. However, nothing is broken. This is really important for you to hear. Broken requires fixing. Healing requires a shift. Broken may not be fixable. Shifting only requires the willingness to explore and consider different perspectives. Fixing is hard. Exploring is interesting. Attempting to fix what is not broken will keep you stuck in the fight or flight cycle.

Get clear on the problem. Detach yourself from the problem and just look at the facts. What is not working in your life right now? What is it that you are thinking or doing that is not working? What is your partner doing? Your boss? Your co-worker? Basically, identify everything that is not bringing you joy, health, success, or love in your life. State it as a fact, without judgment and stories, because whatever negative you choose to focus on will be amplified and made worse. I know I just told you where your focus goes your energy flows. Ultimately, we want to amplify what works rather than what isn't working. However, you first have to identify what is not working before refocusing. Shifting patterns is often difficult, so take baby steps in learning the process. Eventually, you become more efficient at this exploration by bringing awareness and shifting into a more harmonious state without having to spend a great deal of time investigating. For now, indulge yourself the opportunity to fully explore.

The problem is a fact, nothing more. No stories need to build up around it. Do not personalize it. You have a need. What is not working in the situation is only a starting place. In the previous example of financial hardship, what is not working is the amount of income versus the amount of expenses. Your need is to support yourself (and perhaps your family). Perhaps being in that hardship is a way of meeting a deeply subconscious need. Perhaps you need support and nurturing so the subconscious creates an opportunity to make it happen. Unless you are aware of what you are doing, repeating the lesson will be perceived as another painful affirmation of your beliefs. Use the Remembrance practice to identify your heart's desire. Then, get clear on your assets and your expenses to have a true picture of your financial need.

Change will follow your focus, so restate the original question with, "What *is* working in the situation?" In the example, you have the ability to work, the ability to barter, skills or gifts to utilize, a loving family, and the desire to improve the situation. You may even be receiving money without recognizing it; when a friend buys you coffee or a rebate check arrives unexpectedly. When you have invested great time and energy focusing on what is not working, uncovering what is working may be challenging. Find something positive, no matter how small it is. You are still alive and have the power to make choices, so if nothing else, start there.

What would life look like if your situation were in its optimal form? Using the example, you would have the resources to meet your expenses and extra for saving, charitable contributions, and fun! You would be able to support yourself (and your family, if applicable). Let yourself dream of all the possibilities, big and small. The ego will try to interfere in this process by interjecting thoughts such as, "Yeah, but..." and "You tried that before and it didn't work." As well as trying to make you feel guilty or selfishly shameful for allowing yourself to dream and desire. Thank it for its input and go back to dreaming. Use the Remembrance tool to get into your heart and listen to what it can imagine as the optimal form.

What are three solutions that would meet the need and would get you to an ideal situation? In the example, you need to know where you are and where you want to be ideally. You need to determine your true assets and liabilities, and then come up with a plan on how to get from point A to point B. This could be in the form of budgeting, spending less money, finding additional revenue sources, just to name a few. All require an honest look at where you are and how you got to that place.

After identifying the source of the problem and taking steps to change it, seek evidence that the outcome is meeting your needs. In the example, perhaps your income improves, you find more compelling and better paying work that uses your skills. Keep asking yourself, "What is working?" and build on those successes. Keep listening for what you need and seek ways to fulfill those most effectively and efficiently as possible. The problem will diminish on its own. I know that is hard to believe, but it is true.

If a person is the "problem" in your life (or more appropriately a person's behavior), trying to fix the person or behavior only amplifies the negative behavior. Look, no one likes to be told they are wrong or what to do. What if you focused on amplifying what *is* working: the strengths, the positive behavior, the good stuff? Most commonly, negative behaviors are inappropriate ways to meet needs. If you are willing to focus on the persons strengths, love their essence, and risk exploring his or her needs, the bad behavior will shift because it is no longer needed. This is not easy. This takes work. Their hurt inner child and ego will fight this change, just like yours. You are not responsible for healing them. They have to do that work. All you can do is provide the space and a language for such work. If they choose not to heal, you have to choose if you want to stay in that relationship. When you are communicating your needs and feelings and that communication is not reciprocated, growth will be stunted. You have to choose how long you will tolerate being stuck. It is your choice, though.

If you close the book now and don't read a single word past this chapter, your life will be different. Because here's the thing, you have already identified your thinking and the falseness of its protective nature. Once you know that truth, you can never *not* know. That's why they say ignorance is bliss. You are now going to be aware of your thoughts and you have tools to start shifting those thoughts. That's good stuff right there. That is powerful. Yet there is still much to learn. Hold on to your seat because here's where the real fun begins.

Hurt People Hurt

We have spent some time understanding how the brain deals with the disconnection. Now it is time to look at the physiological affect of the disconnection. The mind and body are deeply connected. Your body uses pain and disease (dis-ease) to get your attention. Understanding the body's language unlocks a wealth of wisdom.

When you experience a threat to your existence, real or perceived, the brain prepares the body to take action; to fight, flee, or freeze. The brain has three parts that deal with fight, flight, freeze, and submit (the final stage if the threat persists). The instinctual brain (brain stem) regulates the body in the present moment. The brain stem controls the cardiovascular system alertness, awareness, and consciousness. The emotional brain (limbic system) regulates the endocrine system and autonomic nervous system, including heart and respiratory rate, digestion, salivation, perspiration, diameter of the pupils, and urination. The rational brain (cerebral cortex) is the alert, conscious, logical decision maker that works by organizing information, anticipating and planning. Unfortunately, in high-stress situations, the cerebral cortex is the last to engage as the lower and mid-brain prepare the body for trauma. This makes the ability to process and assess the situation rationally almost impossible.

When faced with a threat, the brain determines whether you need to fight or flee. Heart and respiratory rate increases, pumping adrenaline in preparation to fight or run. Blood is pumped to the largest muscles. Your body's temperature increases and you begin to sweat. This can cause a sensation of cold as the blood flow decreases to the organs and surrounding protective musculature. Everything is on high alert, warning of the impending danger. One of three things occurs: you act upon your instinct to fight or run and survive, the threat passes, or the brain realizes that the trouble is greater than originally perceived.

If the threat is so great that the brain determines your best option is to freeze and hope the threat passes, the body stiffens in preparation for the attack. This is fear at its worst. Have you ever received such shocking news that you literally stood frozen in place? In the animal kingdom, this decreases the chance of being detected. In the human realm, it is similar; if we do not move or make a sound, perhaps the threat will disappear. While the freeze can be momentary, in many situations, a disconnection from the body occurs and everything feels like it is in slow motion. This is a mind trick designed to allow the brain time to process what to do next in order to survive.

There is one more stage: submit. Animals captured by their prey who are not immediately killed will submit. The brain floods the body with endorphins to help numb the body. If the body survives the attack and can flee, the pain of the attack will not be so debilitating. Endorphins are the same chemical produced in extended bouts of exercise, which create what is best known as the "runner's high."

In the best-case scenario of survival, the body instinctually knows how to release the energy created in the fight, flight, freeze, or submit process. Humans and animals release traumatic energy identically. The body begins to shake or tremble. In humans, this is when crying may occur or when you feel that lump in your throat that threatens to cut off oxygen supply between the nose and lungs, preventing you from speaking (or screaming). This is the stage where many people get stuck. Because it is human nature to be supportive of the person experiencing the trauma, we try to calm the person. Some people do not realize this is a natural process and try to stop it. The person in distress is told "suck it up," "be strong," or "get over it". The pattern around the need to be strong and in control causes the ego to create a map in the brain. When a similar situation occurs in the future, the brain reverts back to the need to stop the release of the trauma in order to be strong. By doing this, you essentially trap yourself in the energy of the trauma. The energy remains inside, swirling and swirling. Eventually, it has to go somewhere. We will cover that in a moment.

The final phase of a healthy, normal traumatic energy release is gasping breaths before the heart rate and breathing begin to self-regulate. Have you ever cried, stopped crying, then suddenly after a period of time your body takes a great, gasping breath? This can be almost startling and confusing, because it feels the same as if you were still sobbing. It can also happen as a deep sigh. The breath is regulating the system. The body's processes begin to return to normal. The body will lock in the energy generated by the preparation for trauma, if it is not properly released.

When energy is trapped in the body, the body becomes the enemy. Metaphorically, it is like a tornado in that there is a swirl of energy trapped in you with nowhere to go. The most common symptoms of trapped energy include:
- hyper-arousal
- constriction (respiration, muscle tone, vascular and digestive systems)
- disassociation and denial
- feelings of helplessness
- immobility and freezing
- hyper-vigilance
- intrusive imagery or flashbacks
- extreme sensitivity to light and sound
- hyperactivity
- exaggerated emotional and startle responses
- abrupt mood swings (rage, anger, crying)

- shame
- lack of self-worth
- reduced ability to deal with stress
- difficulty sleeping.

While these may all sound harsh, they can vary from mild to extreme. When they arise, they may make no sense as to why they are the way they are. They can come and go unexpectedly, which is probably the hardest part. One minute you're fine, the next you're a mess. Over time, additional symptoms can develop, such as panic attacks, anxiety, phobias, attraction to and engagement in risky behaviors, addictive behavior, self-mutilation, and the loss of sustaining beliefs (faith). Continued storage eventually transforms into dis-ease and dis-orders in the body.

Dr. John Sarno, pioneer back pain specialist, concluded in his research that repressed emotions, particularly anger, fear, and anxiety, starve muscles of oxygen and cause a wealth of problems in the body. When you tense, the muscles contract and stay contracted. Blood flow and oxygen are constricted. Back pain, peptic ulcer, hiatal hernia, spastic colon, irritable bowel syndrome, hay fever, asthma, prostatitis, migraines, eczema, psoriasis, ringing in the ears, and acne are the examples of dis-ease he discovered formed around emotional repression.

Dr. Peter Levine, trauma healing expert, has identified several diseases and disorders stemming from unreleased traumatic energy, including thyroid malfunctions, environmental sensitivities, headaches, migraines, neck and back problems, chronic fatigue, fibromyalgia, asthma, skin disorders, digestive problems, severe premenstrual syndrome, and frequent urination. Quite an overlap; one set is based on repressed emotions while the other on trapped energy.

In Ayurveda, a form of eastern medicine, chakras, which are more easily understood as energy centers, exist within the body. Think of an electrical power grid. From the power source, electricity is sent through lines to stations where it is then transferred to where it is needed. If everything is working properly, power gets to the proper places. If, for any reason, there is a disruption, power is not delivered. In the body, chakras are like the stations within the power grid. They can expand or contract, impacting the flow of energy. Each chakra is distinct in its function, and it has its own symbol, color, sound and element associated with it. When opened and in balance, there is a harmony that exists both internally and externally within a person. These chakras can close off and trap the energy, too. When that happens, the energy can get a little crazy and cause some problems, sometimes really big problems. Imbalance brings challenges, chaos, and struggles within life and in the health of the individual.

Understanding the responsibilities of the chakras is the key in understanding the trapped energy in the body. The first, or root chakra, deals with our primary caretakers and the ability to be grounded/centered. The second, or sacral chakra, hosts our creativity and sensuality, and relates to all of our chosen relationships. The third, or solar plexus chakra, is our soul's passion, drive, and power. The fourth, or heart chakra, hosts compassion and love. The fifth, or throat chakra, is our truth. The sixth, or the third eye chakra, is our intuition. The seventh and final is the crown chakra, which connects us to a higher power.

Take Dr. Levine's and Dr. Sarno's ailment lists, put them in order of where they are found in the body, and overlap them with the chakra's and you have:

> Root chakra: spastic colon, irritable bowel syndrome, prostatitis, and frequent urination.
> Sacral chakra: irritable bowel syndrome, severe premenstrual syndrome, low back and hip pain (sciatica).

Solar plexus chakra: peptic ulcer, hiatal hernia, and digestive problems including acid reflux. This area also hosts the kidneys, liver, and gallbladder.
Heart chakra: asthma. This area also, obviously, hosts the heart, so cardiovascular issues, and upper back pain around the shoulder blades.
Throat chakra: thyroid malfunction, neck pain, and sore throat.
Third eye chakra: hay fever, migraines, ringing in the ears, TMJ, acne, and headaches.

The body is your alarm system, alerting you that something is askew. Ignore the warnings long enough and all kinds of consequences amass. People can spend years in disease or pain, searching for the answer, spending time, energy, and money on tests, medications, and treatments while the root of the problem goes unexamined. Pain is experienced in layers. You may heal one layer and feel good for a period of time before the subsequent layers, which still need to be healed, begin to surface. You need this period of time to emotionally rest and renew. In fact, the person suffering may even believe they addressed the root cause years ago, yet failed to see how a re-enactment or a trigger brought the root back to life. The process often repeats many times before the real root of the pain is identified and addressed. Perhaps healing that final layer is akin to what the Buddhists call enlightenment.

Fight, flight, freeze, and submit are the physiological responses when your brain utilizes a map, recognizes a pattern, and the ego and essence engage to protect and heal, respectively. In a healthy, balanced person, the fight/flight/freeze/submit response is not habitual and the body is not reflective of the habitual patterns created to survive the hurt of unmet needs. Most commonly, I see imbalance in students and clients as unexplainable back pain, chronic shoulder pain, irritable bowel syndrome (IBS), fibromyalgia, hip pain, a variety of female disorders, and obesity.

For back and hip pain, IBS, and female disorders, I know to ask about troubled or painful relationships, both past and present, including relationships with caretakers. For shoulders and upper back pain, I ask if they feel safe to speak their truth or if they hold back? For weight and fibromyalgia, I ask where do they feel powerless and need to protect themselves? These questions go directly to the stories that keep them stuck.

There are four questions you can ask yourself in times of stress, particularly when you are feeling pain or dis-ease in your body:

What am I fighting or resisting?

From what do I want to run?

What is making me feel paralyzed?

What do I feel like I am submitting to or giving up?

Go into your heart space to do this. Drop down deeply into your heart and ask yourself these questions as you breathe deeply and slowly. Notice what you feel in your body as you ask these questions. What comes up? Be open and willing to risk being surprised. When you have some answers, then you can start investigating your needs and how you can communicate and meet those needs most effectively.

By understanding your needs and feelings, you can save the fight/flight/freeze/submit modes for the real threats, rather than the made-up threats to heal the hurt of unmet needs. When you do experience a true threat, allow yourself the opportunity to process the energy so that it does not remain trapped in the body with its lasting physiological and psychological consequences. As previously mentioned, the Law of Conservation of Energy states that stored (or in this case trapped) energy can change its location or form but cannot be destroyed. If you do not release the traumatic energy, it has to do something; it will be directed internally, externally, or perhaps both.

Violence and trapped energy

I will never forget the night I learned the definition of Ahimsa-non-violence in thought, word, and deed. As I sat in my yoga teacher training, something internal poked me to really process this concept. I wondered if I had violent thoughts. I knew the answer was yes, though I was unsure of the extent. I paid attention over the following days. I was shocked. Not only did I have judgmental thoughts about others and myself, I truly had violent thoughts. In my head, I was so mean to myself. I never would have spoken to someone else as I did to myself. It was truly horrible. Thoughts ranged from the benign "not good enough" chatter to berating myself on my body image, my gifts, my skills, my wisdom, and my abilities. That self-loathing seeped out of me, sometimes flowing, sometimes full-on explosive gushing. No one was good enough for me, including myself! Can you feel how heavy that energy is just reading this?

My words, both internal and external, were unkind. Truth be told, they sometimes still are, though now I am aware and re-harmonize right away. Even my deeds were laced with violence. From undermining myself to not loving unconditionally, from turning my head away from someone who needed help to acting selfishly, and from trying to self-destruct and punish to trying to make others feel that pain, my *behavior* was violent.

There are many ways violence is expressed. Obviously there are single, isolated events such as man made (assault, homicide, harassment, war) and natural acts (tsunami, earthquakes, avalanche). The expression can be explosive. Or, it can be as subtle as words that cut deeply and leave you reeling with pain. Sometimes violence is on-going, such as gang related crime in an impoverished community, living under foreign occupation, or fear of terrorism. Structural violence makes its way into social structures and institutions and causes harm by preventing people from meeting their basic needs. This type of violence is directed at race, class, gender, sexual orientation, age, ethnicity, and geographical origin. Many people refer to this as "social injustice." Structural violence spews into individual violence and feeds on-going man made violence.

Violence can be at a societal level and felt collectively. September 11, 2001 and mass killings are great examples. Even witnessing events from afar can have profound effects, eliciting fear, horror, helplessness, and anger. These emotions impact our thoughts, words, and actions. Stories are formed and shared in circles of family and friends, within the community, and passed down through generations. The impacts of the violence become historical and shape beliefs and identities of entire groups over multiple generations. Cultural violence occurs when an entire group is attacked with the goal of eradicating the group, culture, or ethnicity. The holocaust and genocide are examples. Cultural violence can also have subtle examples around assimilation and loss of cultural identity.

When violence is experienced, the brain immediately shifts into the fight-flight-freeze mode, taking the body on the ride with it in preparation to survive. At this point, many things can happen. The brain stores memories for a mapping process. When the event is over, the emotions of shock, fear, or anxiety arise. Something has changed and there is a loss, be it innocence, heath, trust, or life. Panic arises with awareness of the loss. Strong emotions of anger and rage may surface. Suppression of the emotions occurs in an attempt to numb. There is often an attempt to understand the meaning of the loss, which could bring spiritual questioning. There could be survivor guilt, shame or humiliation. In an attempt to make sense, the subconscious may re-experience the trauma, creating intrusive thoughts or flashbacks. As the conscious mind tries to protect the body from additional pain it causes hyper-vigilance and triggers the desire for avoidance. A sense of safety and security are needed in order to heal, prompting a desire for someone to be held responsible for the hurt. Fantasies of revenge and retribution may develop.

The trapped energy around ahimsa can be expressed outwardly or inwardly. This is called the victim-aggressor cycle. After the initial physiological changes occur, feelings of shock, anxiety, fear, and denial drive a person's desire to be numb. If the pain is directed inward the person may experience feelings of depression, anxiety, shame, hopelessness, internalized oppression, and/or fatalism. This suppression of emotions creates an inner anger or rage that may be temporarily soothed through sex, alcohol, drugs, excessive exercising, and/or self-mutilation. Phobias, chronic pain, and disease can result as chronic suppression occurs. In every sense of the word, the person becomes a victim of self. Even if the person is trying to hide, they suffer silently.

However, if the individual's anger provokes a need for justice or revenge, a belief system of needing to be in control, strong and tough comes into direct conflict with the emotions of fear and anxiety. The ego's need to protect and support the belief system often creates a good-versus-evil narrative. If the person who caused the trauma is "evil" or "bad," then it is justified for bad things to happen to him (or her). A harsh, vindictive act or attack can be made on the attacker, justified in the name of self-defense. That attack can be physical, verbal, or emotional. The victim becomes the aggressor. This behavior becomes increasingly complicated when the original aggressor is not the person the revengeful behavior is acted out against. Examples of this are a child molestation victim who goes on to molest other children, an abused and neglected youth who joins a gang and acts out his or her aggression, or a son of a neglectful mother who grows up to disrespect and distrust women, acting out his aggression on his partner.

Now, please know that I am not talking about a sociopath here. I am referring here to an average person, like you or me, who can act or react violently. In a culture so inundated with violence - in movies, music, video games, and television - is it any surprise the graphic images and words have desensitized the effect on the words you say to yourself? Is it any wonder that our fight-flight-freeze mechanism turns on so frequently that a subconscious addiction develops to the adrenaline constantly surging through the body? Even if someone else isn't creating that perceived threat of attack, you create it for yourself either through thoughts, words, and actions.

Violence happens when the ability to imagine other solutions ceases to exist or when one feels they have no other outlet. Perhaps, on a much deeper level, it is the need for empathy to the deep pain raging within. That pain stems from the flow of Love being cut off and the soul's desperate attempt at re-establish it.

Sometimes, as new layers of pain are discovered, steps of the healing process need to be repeated. Healing is organic and it moves in its own beautiful time, as we are ready. It moves forward, slides backwards, and occasionally gets stuck. There is no manual you can follow and declare, "I'm healed!" You come into this life to experience all emotions and that makes for rich and complex life.

The salve to this violence comes in the form of unconditional love. It is a love that seeks nothing in return. It is understanding without being weak. It is courageous and creative, it seeks good will for all. It allows us to look beyond the hurtful actions of others and allows us to love their essence because we are, like it or not, connected to their essence. By attempting to love unconditionally, you are actually loving yourself unconditionally. Developing and applying this kind of love is a process that might take a lifetime to achieve and yet, even planting the seed in the conscious mind has massive impacts.

Violence is a teacher and guide in its own right. When used as such, the cycles of violence can be broken and a shift towards metta (loving kindness), tolerance, patience, compassion, and forgiveness (for self and others) can occur. It becomes a part of your growth, a reminder of your path and purpose. Now you understand what you are working with or the "why." It is time to break the cycles of violence, re-member your essence, discover YOU, and start to really live the life you came here to live. Let's begin the process of healing.

Part 2: How to get to where your heart desires

The Ultimate Discovery

Who are you? Beyond the roles, the qualities, the characteristics, beyond everything you may think you are, who are you? You are at the part of your journey where you have to *know* that you are something big and that you matter. You are becoming the authentic, Divine version of yourself and that has power. You are part of a bigger picture, a member of the greater family of humanity and of this world.

At your essence is the Energy of Love and as such, you are more than enough and worthy. in order to shift out of you scarcity mentality where you believe there is lack in any area of your life, start observing, listening, and thinking critically about why things are happening in your life and the roles you play in this world. That mentality includes the insanity of greed and intolerance that feeds on your fears. The scarcity mentality is pervasive, constrictive, and destructive. It is the root of suffering because it is separation. It is a living hell. There is a Zen fable on heaven and hell:

> One night, during dinner, a powerful, revered samurai walked into the dining hall. Seeing his favorite Zen teacher, he said, "Sensei! I have been sharing with my brothers about the lessons you taught us. Speak to us of the nature of heaven and hell." The Zen master never looked up from his soup, but said, "You? You are a vile, disgusting, miserable being. Your mother must be ashamed. Why do you think you are worthy enough that I should tell you anything?" Consumed by rage, the samurai draws his sword, raising it to cut off the master's head. The Zen master looks up and says, "This is hell."
>
> Instantly, the samurai understood that he had just created his own hell: dark, raging, filled with hatred, ego, pride,

anger, and resentment. He recognized that he was so entrenched in hell that he was ready to kill someone he respected. He dropped his sword and fell to his knees. Tears filled his eyes as he put his palms together to bow in gratitude for this insight. The Zen Master then said, "This is heaven."

You already know that the disconnection from your energy of Love created stories that evolved into limiting beliefs. Staying stuck is actually a choice. Day in and day out, you choose: accountability and responsibility or blame and victimhood, anger and loathing or limitless and joy, heaven or hell. Heaven and hell are not something that happen after death, they are *now*. Ralph Waldo Emerson said that the ancestor of every action is thought. The power of the mind is greater than any weapon and more secure and stronger than any prison because it needs no walls or locked gates to imprison. And yet, the mind has the capacity to heal better than any physician or medication.

In the song "Closer To Fine," the Indigo Girls sing: "Darkness has a hunger that's insatiable and lightness has a call that's hard to hear." That appetite is within your soul, as it is in all souls. Injustice, tyranny, greed, and bias are all justifiable causes for the wars fought in this world, yet those qualities are not solely "out there" in other people. They are within you and me and everyone. They shape our thoughts. These thoughts are energy that attracts like-energy. The energy grows collectively and shapes the global environment. Battles continue to rage on, with the greatest battle being fought in your own soul. You cannot push this battle onto others, blaming or shaming them into ownership. Peace starts within your own being. One of my teachers taught me to not mind what I cannot control, let all be what it is meant to be, and learn from the shadows without judging. Emotions are simply energy. As you feel a particularly charged emotion, all it means is that there is content attached to you, some illusion or limitation you have created. If you created it, guess what? You can uncreate it, too. It is your continual choice, moment-by-moment, day-in and day-out: heaven or hell. That choice is how you slay the fear that keeps you stuck.

Within everyone are shadow and light qualities. Shadow qualities include: fear, annoyance, anger, aversion, confusion, disconnection, chaos, shame, fatigue, pain, sadness, tension, vulnerability,, and the derivatives of each emotion. Light qualities include: compassion, affection, engagement, hope, confidence, security, joy, excitement, gratitude, inspiration, abundance, peace, trust, renewal, and all their derivatives. Your ability to experience both the shadow and light qualities are truly a Divine gift. You are a container with enough room to hold *all* the qualities. When you are disconnected, you forget this and your focus becomes limited to a few qualities such as joy. When you place judgment on the shadow qualities, trying only to feel the light qualities, your soul will poke at you, reminding you, "You are that!" What you resist will persist. This is the importance of balance. Until you embrace the totality of you, that you are the energy of all emotions, you stay stuck in the prison of the mind.

Within you resides all the cosmos, all the answers, and the seeds of all beings interconnected as One. Sohum, a Sanskrit (the oldest existing language) word, describes this well. Sohum means, I am that; co-creation and destruction, light and darkness, war and peace, love and fear." Who is this great I Am within? As sohum you are the sun: a masculine energy providing warmth, energy, light and life. You are the moon: a feminine energy that provides guidance through the darkness, rest, reprieve, and healing. You are the elements. Fire; burning anything that does not serve or harmonize in the energy of Love on the sacred journey. Water; fluid, soft, and flexible, capable of transforming the most rigid surfaces, and washing pure the dark spots of the soul. Earth; the sacred ground, a place for seeds to be sown and fruit to be reaped (both shadow and light). While solid, the earth is constantly changing and shifting, expanding and contracting. Air; the breath, invisible, yet everywhere, and always shared. You have the ability to stand still and become the collective consciousness, aware of what is happening all around you, all at once simply by breathing in and out consciously. I know, deep, huh? Just take it in. Maybe you get it now, or maybe the knowledge is a seed being planted somewhere in the recesses of your mind to grow later into a full understanding. It is all energy!

Sohum makes you an instrument of truth, healing, and growth. You are the eyes through which the Divine sees all life and all realms of possibility. Even if you do not believe in "God," you have the power to experience this life in its fullest, choosing moment by moment to see the best or worst in every person, place or thing you encounter. Your choice will bring great pleasure or discomfort, so choose wisely. You are a sacred witness, both to yourself and others, honoring the experiences that shape the opportunity to Love and transcend. You are a reminder of Home, the sacred space that serves as refuge, the place to fully become authentic regardless of the inequities that mire your mind. Sohum calls you to be Justice, not judgment. This is about being clear, impartial, favoring or hating no one, taking in the facts, tapping into your Divine, infinite Knowing and seeking a way to heal the hurt. Sohum makes you everything, all at once, limitless and expansive. That is powerful. Most people are afraid of being powerful and using the unconditional energy of Love in this life.

Your duty is to unconditionally love those people you come in contact with *every* day, from the briefest moment to the deepest relationship. This goes for the people you like or love, as well as those who challenge you, maybe *especially* for those who challenge you. The most important person you are called to love is YOU, all of you, especially the parts of you that you have judged, hated, been frustrated with, tried so hard to change. To fulfill your duty, you must examine what makes you feel good. What is the energy behind what makes you feel good? Practice reciprocity of that delight and energy. Give the energy back to the world, to the people around you, and most importantly to yourself tenfold: a smile, a compliment, saying something positive, a kind and unselfish act. This is what I Am is all about; reciprocity of the energy of Love, baby!

All life is in you and you are in all life. That means your soul wants to exchange the highest vibration of energy, the energy of Love, with others. The soul must dance and it will persist until you are broken open in the middle of a battle or in the arms of a lover. So you must practice justice, compassion, and forgiveness not only for others, but also for yourself. You create and destroy. You fear and love. You are light *and* darkness. All from one moment to the next because you are *that* I Am. You become a sensuous lover of life because you are vulnerable enough to feel and be. You are intuitive so choose to listen closely to your inner voice. Doing so allows you to see and attract the energy of Love in others. As an only child, I knew the truth behind how fun it could be to play alone with only my imagination keeping me company. It was always more fun to play with others, and their imaginations contributed to the party. Energetically playing together now in the flow of Love is beyond words. It is simply fun.

Embracing sohum is the ultimate sovereignty. You can be autonomous because you *know* your self and your power. No one can control you because you *know* the difference between the soul and the rigid ego. You can see other people's limitations and illusions and you no longer have to play in that realm. There can be no controlling influence over you because you *know* that heaven and hell are of your own making and ultimately you choose where you reside. You have conviction. The only supreme power over you is the shared Divine, infinite energy of Love that you know is within all, even if others do not acknowledge or recognize it within themselves.

To be the highest version of yourself, aim for balance in your thoughts, words and actions: strength with gentleness, action with stillness, integrity with forgiveness, light with shadow, and purity with experience. The average person will believe this is crazy. You, however, are not average. Their judgment no longer matters. Every time you fall out of balance, the lesson will cross your path again until you finally temper it through the energy of Love, in order to create balance. Repeating that lesson with your present knowledge will be exponentially heavier and more difficult each time. Is that something you need or desire to do?

Your initiation into *your* authenticity has some requirements. Start taking responsibility for your own emotions and needs, as well as for your thoughts, words, and actions. Be willing to accept all emotions without attachment or judgment because nothing is permanent and all emotions are simply energy. Without attachment, the emotion can be experienced and then dissolves into the next experience. Understand your intentions behind your thoughts, words, and actions. When you live consciously, you live from a place of integrity. Passing the buck on your responsibility, blaming others for your experience is a surefire way to repeat the lesson. As you practice awareness, and it does take practice, you start to ask yourself, "Where is this coming from - my ego or soul?"

As mentioned before (and worth repeating), you soul is clear and precise when responding to that question and feels open in the body whereas the ego rationalizes, brings in the doubt and fear, and feels constricted in the body. Once you know where you are coming from, proceed appropriately; heal what needs to be healed, meet your needs more effectively, and risk being vulnerable. Be open to curiosity. Allow yourself to take risks. Be creative. You are the artist of your life. Even if you never pick up an art tool, you are creating your great masterpiece by what you think, say, and do. Creation is life generating and abundant, whereas fear and scarcity are destructive. Choose to co-create with the energy of Love.

As you engage these actions, you re-member as you are re-connecting to your essence. No more disconnection. Once you know it, you cannot forget and if you choose to disconnect again, it will be a direct trip back into the depths of hell. With awareness and consciousness, your trips to this less than desirable state are shorter. You can self-correct the journey and learn a little more from each lesson, heal another layer of hurt, and uncover your authenticity. Living authentically is strong, exciting, and such an adventure. You are able to finally live your purpose because you are not living for others or stuck in the cycle of repeating lessons. I call that liberation. What will you do with that freedom?

Healing Hurt

To heal the hurt, the heart and the mind both have to take a journey. The healing process in the journey is organic in that the components may not play out in any particular order. For that reason, remain flexible and open, be willing to be surprised, and be okay with what may feel like setbacks. What feels like backsliding to the mind is just another layer of pain being addressed, an awareness of disharmony, and an opportunity to bring love and acceptance. The ego will judge this as bad, saying "Here we go again!" Now you have the tools to process the pain. It is important to know that your time with the emotional charge will be shorter. Your choices will be different because you know how to identify what is really happening.

Are you willing to feel your pain and all of the shadow emotions associated with that pain without judging those feelings, the situation or the person(s) involved? You are the energy of Love. *Seeking* love is unnecessary; you already have it. Your job is to remove the obstacles that block the flow of Love's energy. Holding on to the hurt builds barriers to the Love within you and all around you. You built these barriers to protect against the hurt, the unmet expectations, the unmet needs, but ultimately the barriers do not resolve the pain. In fact, they keep the pain on life support. Many times when you look at the facts of the story, you can see how small the situation really was that caused the pain. At other times, the situations were life-altering experiences such as death, hate crimes, or child abuse. The principles rooted in Love can help with both large and small situations, though greater assistance is sometimes needed to process the trauma.

The first part of the healing process is for the mind. This process comes from the work of Olga Botcharova. Previously I discussed the cycles of violence and how traumatic energy plays out in the

94

body by your internalizing or externalizing the pain. Breaking free takes time and is unique to each person. As you recognize and begin to accept the loss, your awareness of the depth and gravity of the loss may come in waves. At first you may see the obvious changes: in a break-up the relationship and all the routines with it are gone; in an argument, the ability to be open or trust may be wounded; in the loss of a job, the income, security, and routine are gone. Then you begin to see the less obvious impacts of loss, all leading to a disconnection from the energy of Love. Needs go unmet, and pain is rooted. A key step in breaking free of the cycle is acceptance which takes time and guidance.

Before you can start the process to go that deeply, you need to feel safe. Safety is more than physical; it is also spiritual and emotional. Being hurt can knock you off center. You need to have some time to return to center. Pain is so raw when it happens that having it in your face can simply be too overwhelming. You need quiet some space and a place to retreat. You may have experienced at some point wanting to sleep or you've had difficulty getting out of bed after a significant loss. Your body and mind are trying to shelter you. Healing is a vulnerable space. You need to feel safe with the people around you with whom you share your thoughts and fears.

If you do not feel safe, you will not heal. You will get stuck in the cycles of violence. Seek ways to feel safe. Many people lean into their faith to find safety. Religious or spiritual rituals, prayer, wisdom and comfort from spiritual texts or music can help. Spending time in nature also helps. Experiencing those moments of grace that happen after a loss allows you to have a taste of faith and a soulful connection- a knowing that you are not alone. Community strength can also provide safety. In a supportive community, people provide resources, nurturing, protection and privacy. They also gather to share stories, offering wisdom and empathy, decreasing the sense of being isolated in the situation. Reflecting on the painful situation naturally occurs. You can choose to internalize it and allow the pain to grow or you and neutralize it by getting it out of your head.

You will likely find yourself exploring what led up to the painful experience. Exploration is the place where many people get stuck. Unwilling to understand the root causes or hear the "enemy's" story, you get caught in the desire to have your pain recognized, validated, and healed. You fail to look at your own shortcomings in the situation (this does not apply for victims to hate crimes and child abuse). Blame, shame, and guilt can come out in full force. However, when you start exploring how you were meeting your needs in that situation, how you were making choices that enabled the hurtful behavior, you can seek ways to meet your needs more effectively, efficiently, and with far less cost. If you are willing to do that, you sever the energetic bond that remains through retelling your victim story. Instead, you attract future opportunities to repeat the pain in some way in order to heal the pain of those unmet needs.

You have a choice; stay a victim or risk moving forward. Remaining a victim has its payoff as discussed previously. So does being willing to move past the blame, taking responsibility for your part, and moving from surviving to thriving. In doing so, you practice tolerance. You are willing to endure the temporary hardship because you want to move beyond the stuck state. You have to co-exist, if not with the person who hurt you, with the experience of the loss. You cannot take that experience back. It is now woven into the fabric of your history. You have the choice not to let it define you. Are you willing to break the patterns of learned helplessness or hopelessness?

You may not even be conscious of these patterns. Being helpless brings attention, comfort, caring, all of which feel good. If being in pain or being a victim is the most effective way you have found to meet those needs, you can see how easily it can become a pattern.

As you face your pain, look at what *you* did or failed to do in the situation. With a few exceptions such as child abuse and hate crimes, both parties play some role. Take accountability for your part. Be brutally honest with yourself. It is one of the hardest and most empowering things you will do in the process of healing.

Identify your needs and how you chose to meet them (or not if you put the responsibility on someone else). Your needs being met is the "why" certain things keep happening the way they do. As you progress with awareness, you will recognize your familiar behaviors of attempting to meet your needs and be able to pivot into more effective, more efficient, and less costly ways of meeting your needs. Self-awareness brings insight into the previously confusing behavior of others. You can cut through the red herring arguments to get to the core issues. You can look beyond the bad behavior, without excusing it, and identify the motivation behind the behavior.

Begin to create a story that promotes lasting healing. Who are you now that this painful experience has happened? At your core, you are still the energy of Love. Only you can decide how you will integrate the experience and move forward. Once you have answered that question, you can engage offenders with an open heart and perhaps hear *their* story. Their story may not be as evolved or enlightened as yours and that can be frustrating, perhaps even creating an energetic charge in you that takes you back into the process. Experiencing this setback is simply another opportunity to engage self-love, compassion, nurturing and re-connection to Love's energy and flow. Or you may be able to hear each other's stories, start negotiating solutions and seek ways to integrate the hurt into your new story and identity. Perhaps you are able to reconcile. It is perfectly okay if you choose not to. The sacred contract between the two of you may be over and it is time to move on. Listen to your heart for direction.

Healing the hurt in a way that moves you out of the victim-aggressor cycle develops resiliency. You empower yourself to heal. The next time you hurt, lean into and engage your pain. You will develop empathy with others who are experiencing a similar hurt. Your experience of overcoming adversity can be inspiring and educational to someone who is buried in their pain.

The next part of the healing process is for the heart. In times of stress, you emotionally revert back to the age you first experienced a serious disconnection or trauma. If you pay attention, you will notice qualities of a child in your reactions (or inactions as may be the case). An emotional developmental disability has occurred. Being unconscious of this emotional stuck point can be challenging in relationships. Communication with you can be very confusing if your inner child's age is four and you tend to yourself express through a tantrum, or seven and you sulk, or nine and you become petulant. You may even notice that your behavior confuses you. It took me a long time to recognize my four-year-old behavior and then it took even longer to know what to do with it.

The child inside of you serves as a guide by presenting you an opportunity to meet the needs the your inner child has been longing for. Just like you would care for a hurt child in real life, care for this wounded child in your heart. Your child needs to feel safe to communicate. If you have repressed or ignored your child for a long time, it may take some time for him or her to know you are serious about finally listening. When you first start communicating with your child, it truly takes just showing up, being tender, and compassionate. Ask what is needed to feel safe enough to be free, play, and dream again. Being present for the child is often enough to earn the child's trust and create a sense of safety. Both of which are needed for healing. Ask what would make the child feel supported, important, and that the child matters? Get to know this child. Playing is the best way to do this. What does he or she love to do? Get lost in the moment like you used to at that age. Have fun.

Explore. Be silly. Listen. Let your love flow. What would make the child feel appreciated and connected? Commit to providing for your child.

You and your inner child become a team. The child will let you know when you are getting close to your emotional edges as it begins to react. You can then explore together what is needed to move forward together. The more aware you become, the faster you see the signals and know it is time to take a breath and employ the tools you have. This process becomes quicker and quicker each time you do it. I know you would love to just get rid of the flash of anger and the foot-stomping, arm-crossing purely defiant inner child. Remember, you resisted listening to this child for years. Embrace, accept, and use the child as your guide. You will find yourself centering much faster with each experience together.

Children with "owies" find great solace from a Bandaid and kiss. An emotional first aid kit serves that purpose for immediately easing your hurts. In addition to all of the tools previously covered, here are two additional tools that can be used instantly and discreetly when you feel pain, fear, anger, and sadness. You could also use these when you feel off balance, challenged, or emotionally charged. The first tool is attention to the breath. When you are stressed, the breath shortens and becomes shallow as the muscles tense, making it difficult for oxygen flow to the muscles. Without proper distribution of blood flow and oxygen, carbon dioxide and other toxins cannot be removed. Toxins are stored and the muscles are starved of necessary oxygen. Eventually tension turns to pain.

Take a deep breath right now. Deeper. Slower. Ease the tension in your shoulders and hands. Try to make the next breath even deeper, slower, and longer. Notice what is happening in the body as the breath flows in and out. This is the simplest breath in yoga:

- Breathing in, allow the top of the chest, the diaphragm and the lower belly to expand.
- Exhaling, allow the belly to fall as the air is pushed completely out of the body.
- Start with trying to inhale for five full seconds, pausing, and then exhaling for five full seconds with a pause before beginning again.
- Six rounds of this breathing would last one minute.
- Then, try to hold the end of the exhalation for a longer and longer period of time. This resets the oxygen and carbon dioxide balance in the body. Avoid holding the top of the inhalation because a natural response in the flight-fight-freeze mode is to inhale sharply and hold the breath. You are working to get yourself out of that pattern.

This breathing technique can be used by itself or combined with other tools. Another breathing technique is to rest the tip of the tongue behind the upper teeth, allowing your lips to part slightly. Inhale through the nose and exhale through the mouth as if you are blowing out a candle.

The second tool is finger holds. Eastern medicine has identified many meridians in the body through which energy travels. In the hand, each finger has a meridian and each meridian is connected to an organ in the body. Strong emotions can overpower the meridians because emotions are a form of energy and travel throughout the body through the meridians. Holding the finger associated with the emotion helps to slow the emotional energy and calm both the body and mind. Each finger is also associated with an element in nature. The elements can be particularly helpful in centering and gaining clarity in difficult times.

Finger	Element	Emotion
Thumb	Fire	Grief, pain, sadness
Index finger	Air	Fear, panic
Middle finger	Ether	Anger, rage, resentment
Ring finger	Earth	Worry, anxiety
Pinky finger	Water	Self-confidence, self-esteem

Simply hold the appropriate finger with the opposing hand for 3-5 minutes while breathing intentionally. Imagine the emotional charge draining out of the finger. You will probably feel a pulse in the finger that slows over time. Notice what you need in that moment. What does your heart desire emotionally? As you inhale, allow your heart to fill with that quality. For example, if you are worried, identify what you are longing for: courage, security, safety, appreciation, or connection. Inhale and imagine that quality expanding. Exhaling, send gratitude to the charged emotions for allowing you the opportunity to go deeper into your heart and really explore what you need most in that moment. Breathe in the quality your heart longs for and breathe out gratitude. Notice the shift that occurs.

Healing returns you to the path of your purpose in this life. You are the stone thrown into the calm water of life, creating a ripple into your immediate circle and into an ever widening circle of influence. You are an example, whether you like it or not! While you must speak your truth and hold space for others to do the same, there is a distinct difference between tapping into shared or similar grief and healing versus tapping into grief to inflame or ignite a spirit of vindication, revenge, and destruction.

You will not always know the impact you make on others. You will, however, always know that you have responsibilities because you own the gift of sacred memory. That is why you picked up this book. Even if someone encouraged you read it, you could have refused. Something nudged you subconsciously. That sacred memory of who you are is triggered by your essence begging to live fully and intentionally. You will be leaned on and called upon at times, until you feel you have nothing left to give. Yet you must give more, at the very least to yourself. This process starts by healing the hurt and then opening the channel of Love with forgiveness to allow the energy to flow.

In healing yourself, you help heal others. You give them the inspiration and the space to take that first courageous step. They see you survived and can tell the tale. "Soul Meets Body," a song by Death Cab For Cutie, says, "I know our filthy hands can wash one another's and not one speck will remain." Ultimately, this is your gift and power. It is time to fall in love with the greatness that is YOU, unconditionally loving yourself, releasing the need to be right or to blame others for your inadequacies. You *are* strong because you are willing and able to feel, accept, and love. The battles you fight from this point forward will ultimately allow the energy of Love to flow in the world, co-creating abundance.

Letting Go

The energy of Love is unshakably restless until it successfully harmonizes all remaining pain into the stream of unconditional Love, all scars into beauty, all shame into the grace of humor. Lessons repeat until they are learned. Even then, with so many layers of pain, the lessons may recreate in a slight variation in order to help you transform into living authentically. Letting go is about surrendering; releasing the need to be right, validated, vindicated, or remain a victim. Forgiveness is a powerful tool of letting go.

Shift your perspective when it comes to pain. The people who have most hurt you have also been helping you to grow. Certainly I would love to have fewer challenges and more inspired growth. I suspect you would, too. Hurting sucks. Struggling sucks. Awareness of scared contracts takes you from wondering why something has happened to you to questioning whose lesson is it really? When I learned about sacred contracts, I asked myself if it was my contract to grow as the emotionally abandoned child of a mother with mental illness? Or am I here to help her with her lessons and growth? Or is it both of our lessons? This shift may not make you feel any better about the situations that caused such pain, nor am I asking you to be pious and forget it happened. It is simply a shift in perspective that may allow the energy to be redirected in a way that removes stuckness, self-sabotage, cycles of violence, guilt, blame, and shame.

When you make a scared contract, you make it in order to learn and experience the Divine qualities more fully; experiencing both shadow and light, abundance and scarcity of the qualities. There are many, many Divine qualities. This is a short list:

mercy	benevolence
purity	faith
peace	creativity/creation

beauty	forgiveness
giving	openness
knowledge	wisdom
humility	vision
discernment	justice
magnificence	gratitude
unconditional love	preservation
nourishment	generosity
witness	truth
trust	strength
protection	connection
compassion	guidance
patience	destruction.

Each of these qualities have shadow and light aspects. They each come with an antagonistic quality, for example creation and destruction. Both can be beneficial or a hindrance depending on the use of the quality. Depending on the situation, the abundance or scarcity of the quality could be positive or negative. However, these qualities are simply an expression of energy. For me, there are many on this list that I see woven through my experiences, yet unconditional love is the one that stands above all the others. You will begin to see a theme through your life that as you explore your needs, one quality will stand out for you. As you recognize this quality, you seek ways to engage it more in your life instead of turning your face from its sacredness. Your connections will deepen; your patterns will dissolve or evolve. Healing can really take root when you embrace the totality of these qualities.

We all have moments of Divine connection. The moment I realized I did not love myself was a Divine connection. It's often hard to explain the experience of Divine connection. For me, it is usually a voice I hear or an idea that resonates through my body. Realizing I had to write this book was a Divine moment of connection. When you meet someone and you feel like you have known them before is a moment of Divine connection. Sometimes the moment presents itself through the line of a song that you have heard a thousand times but suddenly this line hits you like a two by four up-side the head. It could be the interview you stumble on when changing radio stations. Often they are subtle moments that evolved into profound experiences.

Entering into the contract is essentially agreeing to challenge or be challenged, most likely through pain. If I knowingly agree to help you learn that lesson through a painful experience, my spirit must have a great deal of love and admiration for yours. As we process through life and the various stakeholders begin to fulfill contracts, without any memory of the contract, it is easy to move into the "good versus bad" narratives, straight into victimhood, needs being unfulfilled and the armor and walls get acquired as protection from pain. Cycles begin.

My relationship with my mother is a good example because it is the same skeleton of a story that clients and friends have shared over the years. My mother seemed to have abandoned me shortly after I was born. It took me decades to understand it was *her* deep-seated fear of abandonment that caused her to act in a way that frightened our family and caused my grandparents to step in and take care of me. It was not because she did not love me. Quite the contrary, she loved me very much. She did not, however, love herself. When I was four, her mother passed away and my mom was left, unprepared, to become a full-time mom. I spent decades worrying about being abandoned as she tilted between manic and depressive in waves of undiagnosed bi-polar disease, sometimes emotionally present and often emotionally buried and distant.

As a child, this was terribly confusing and I spent most of that time wondering what I had done to make her angry or sad and what I could do to make her happy. Eventually, the wondering turned into anger. There was a child in me that believed I was so unlovable that the people I loved would leave me. It was the underlying belief that affected all of my relationships. I realized, eventually, that this fear was built on a false premise. As an adult, I realized that no one could abandon me because I am capable of caring for myself. That, plus the knowledge that she did not love herself, allowed me to shift my perspective and gain a confidence that positively benefitted all my relationships. She needed me to love her unconditionally so that she could find the way to love herself. I have come to believe that my life lesson is how to love and be loved unconditionally. Any wonder she and I chose this go-around together?

You know you are in a sacred contract when faced with situations that require unaccustomed skills, courage, and/or wisdom. The exact moment you know you are fully engaged feels like the cosmic 2 x 4 upside your head, dropping you to your knees, making you plead, "I don't know how to do this." Your brain doesn't have to know the "how." That knowledge is inherently in your soul. You simply have to be quiet, re-member, and listen. Your heart and soul will guide you. How you respond to the situation that is stretching and straining your every fiber of being is up to you. You have free will to stay stuck and repeat the lesson. You can also choose to face the challenge even if you fear that you do not know how to face it.

Your battles generate enormous energy. That energy can be trapped in your body or released and transformed. Most fights and disagreements are not really about the surface issue, rather some need not being met. Sometimes you will catch that in the moment and sometimes it comes in hindsight. When you reflect back, ask yourself, "Did I do everything I could to meet my needs effectively? Did I fight for Love or ego? How could I have loved unconditionally in that moment?" These questions bring great insight if you are willing to be honest. Perhaps not today, or tomorrow, but rest assured the lesson will return and you must be prepared.

There is a confession of sins in the Episcopal Church's *Book of Common Prayer*, "We confess that we have sinned against thee in thought, word, and deed, by what we have done and what we have left undone." In the confession, the need to look at what we have left undone is as important to bring harmony as for what we have actually done. This is about:

Saying no when you mean yes, or yes when you mean no.
Settling
Ignoring the pain of others
Pride
Getting the last word
The need to be right at all costs
Not listening
Not hearing
Not reaching out for help when you needed it
Turning your back on someone who reached out for help
Judging
Having contempt towards another
Manipulating
Dishonesty (whether it was a blatant lie or lying by omission)
Not being authentic
Second-guessing yourself and others
Reacting as your inner child
Sleepwalking through life
Compromising your integrity and honor
Overlooking injustice
Living in fear
Holding on to anger, shoving it below the surface
Being violent (in thought, word, or deed)
Not caring (about yourself or others)
Being a chameleon
Not living in the present
Blaming, shaming, and guilting others
Obsessing

Trying to change anyone other than yourself
Wasting time
Building and believing in faulty mental models
This is a short list. We are human; we will win some and lose some in our quest for living authentically. It is what you do with those wins and losses that make such a difference.

Everything starts within. You play a role in every experience, whether you like it or not. Therefore, you must be accountable for your part. Taking responsibility requires you to honestly look at what was done to you, what you did, and what you failed to do in moments of conflict.
Thomas Merton, Trappist monk, mystic and author said, "Peace demands the most heroic labor and the most difficult sacrifice. It demands greater heroism than war. It demands greater fidelity to the truth and a much more perfect purity of conscience."
Forgiveness brings liberation from the repeated cycles of violence. Forgiveness takes courage.

Who do you need to forgive? Forgiveness does not mean forgetting, nor does it mean condoning hurtful actions or words. Forgiving is "for giving": love to yourself, liberation, space, and healing. Self-forgiveness is the greatest gift you can give yourself. There are two forgiveness meditations that I use with clients, a version of the Hawaiian forgiveness ritual called Ho'ono Pono Pono and a Buddhist meditation called Metta, or loving kindness. Both are about shifting negative energy to compassion. You can do these anytime and anyplace. The person does not even need to know you are doing them. They are, in fact, more for you than them.

Begin the Ho'ono Pono Pono ritual by bringing to mind one person you wish to forgive. Take some time to write out all your grievances with the person who you seek to forgive. Lay it all out there. This person will never read what you wrote. List all the ways they hurt you, everything that made you angry or disappointed.

And equally important, list all the ways you are angry with yourself.

When that feels complete, center yourself with a few calming breathes. Bring to mind the *essence* of the person with whom you need to do the clearing. Imagine them standing in front of you. Look the person in the eyes. Look beyond their human form into their essence. They have a core that connects to the universe and all who are in it. You are looking into that raw space inside of them that they try to protect with their armor or walls. Remember, bad behavior is the language of the deeply wounded. Tell them, "I forgive you." Then share what you forgive. There is no reason to hold back. This is your time to let go of everything. What has angered you, saddened you, caused you fear?

Now thank this person if for no other reason than for agreeing to help you on this journey through this process of growth. Pain is an awesome teacher. Thank this person for the being in this space and time, for that lesson. What else about this person are you grateful for? Gratitude is incredibly powerful. It is how to super-size your healing. When you express gratitude, you are telling the Universe that you are open to receiving. That is why gratitude is a part of this process.

Tell the person you are sorry. Own *your* responsibility in the situation. We often remain energetically bonded through our victimhood by repeating the story, casting blame, shame and guilt, or even by holding onto anger. Acknowledging your role helps you break free. What else are you sorry for?

Finally, say, "I love you." This could be the hardest part. You are not agreeing to forget, nor are you agreeing to like the person or even re-engage in any form of relationship with the person. You are not loving their actions or behavior. Loving the essence of the person allows you space to love yourself, to heal yourself, and consequentially, heal others. This is critical.

Now, repeat the process, forgiving, thanking, loving and apologizing to your Self.

You may finish by saying the following prayer if you choose:

> Divine Creator, I am willing to release any and all energy associated with pain, fear, anger, sadness or shame. I am willing to open and shift the energy between myself and (insert name of other person). Cleanse me and ____ now of any remaining harmful energetic connections to this sacred contract. I am willing to release this pain and return to the energy of Love NOW! I am willing to be free. I am willing to allow ___ to be free. IT IS DONE! With infinite love and gratitude, thank you.

Take a few moments, with your eyes closed, imagining a violet flame in front of you, consuming any remaining darkness, pain, anger, or hatred. When you are ready, slowly open your eyes and return to the room. Take your piece of paper that you wrote your grievances and either safely burn it or tear it up and hold the pieces under water for a minute before discarding.

With Metta, you bring three people into your mind's eye: one you adore, one that is an acquaintance whom you do not know well but like, and the third is a person who challenges you. In your mind, bring each to stand in front of you, one at a time to perform the meditation. You will take turns speaking to each person, one at a time, bringing each to stand directly in front of you, and they return the words back to you before inviting the next person into your circle. To the one you adore (and they to you), say:
"May you be happy.
May you be healthy.

May you be free from fear.
May you have peace."

As you say the words to one another, a light connects your hearts.
The light remains connected as you bring in your acquaintance
and repeat the words to one another. Once this is performed and
all three hearts are connected, the three of you will welcome in
your challenging person. As you bring the challenging person to
the group, see beyond their actions to their essence, to the person
who has experienced hurts, disappointments, and triumphs, just
like you. See how their fear influences their behavior. After you
finish with the challenging person, allow all three people to fade
until you are standing face-to-face with yourself. Repeat the words,
looking into your own eyes. Stay for a moment with the sensation
before coming out of the meditation.

Both of these are powerful forgiveness meditations. Both can be
used instantly in any moment by shortening them into a chant.
    I forgive you. Thank you. I am sorry. I love you.
Or:
    May you be happy, healthy, free from fear, and have peace.

No one needs to know you are doing these mantras. You can be
engaged in a conversation, repeating the words as a mantra or
prayer with each breath. I am always amazed at how calm this
practice makes me when I am in a challenging discussion. I often
notice a change in the other person, too. Perhaps it is nothing more
than me remaining calm or perhaps their energy really does shift.
Either way, the important thing is that the situation loses its charge
and allows healthy communication to occur.

Pain layers on itself, particularly when patterns are repeated. For
each layer, you may need to repeat this process, sometimes many
times, in order to really penetrate those layers. When a relationship
ended shortly before I learned the Ho'Ono ritual, my mind

alternated between "what if" and angry revenge. I recognized that my pride was significantly bruised and my ego was hurt. I started practicing these forgiveness rituals towards my ex and myself. Once was not enough. Every time another layer was uncovered, the ego would remind me of all my false beliefs around not being good enough and being unlovable. Two times... three times... six times before the painful layers were salved and my ego realized there was nowhere left to dwell. Now, in the rare moments when my ego tries to bring it up, I simply go into the shortened version and just take a minute to ask myself what is really hurting and what needs are not being met?

Just because a charge remains does not mean that healing is not occurring. Rather, it simply means that another layer is ready to release the charge. Eventually, all stories, energy, and pain around you cease to hold you hostage and cease to affect other areas in your life. You may even find that as you release your charge around the person, their behavior shifts. Even if their behavior does not change, the release of energy allows *you* the strength to be present in your life and hold true to your needs, desires, and values without compromise, guilt, fear, or shame. Sometimes, you will need to seek assistance. Even just telling the Divine and your guides that you need help will set in motion bring to you exactly who you need for assistance. The pain can be too deep or too challenging to face alone. There is nothing wrong with asking for help! Asking for help is a form of courage because it proves you are trying to bring healing.

There are some things that you simply cannot plow through, try as you might, and letting go is one of those. The process of letting go reminds me of when I went four-wheeling with a friend in the desert. We took a road, which got smaller and smaller and the walls of a canyon closed in on us the further we went. Eventually we were at the end of the path, the road long gone, stopped by a wall of boulders. I could see that there were openings in the boulders where water, animals, and even a hiker could get through. Obviously, the water had it the easiest, soft and pliable, it could slip through many spaces. The animals, depending on size, could pass rather easily, too. The hikers would have more of a challenge. In your life, you have the choice of being the driver of the truck, the hiker, an animal, or the water when it comes to conflict transformation. The driver has to go backwards, down the path to the road and a bit further before turning around to find another road. Trying to plow through the healing process is a bit like that; you usually have to back out and find a totally different road to take. When you plow through, chances are you will find yourself repeating the lesson. As a hiker or animal, you will repeat the cycle of progressing then getting stuck as you negotiate your options. Your will to get through the narrow pass in challenging situations will often blind you to the more intuitive options available. That is why it is important to pause, breathe, and listen to your intuition. If you try to plow through the challenge and just "get over it," the ego will create shameful beliefs in attempt to make sense of the pain:

> I will never be enough
> It's not safe to be me
> I am always left out or last to be picked
> I will always be abandoned
> Speaking out is not safe
> No matter how hard I try, it's never enough
> Life's not fair
> Being powerful/successful/rich/outgoing is bad
> I am unworthy
> I am undeserving
> Suffering and hardship prove I am worthy
> I'm not important
> I don't matter
> I am unlovable
> I'll always end up alone

Did any of those resonate with you? These beliefs separate you from the interconnectedness of life. They disconnect us from our own essence and the energy of Love. These beliefs set up the maps that subconsciously drive your decisions. These are the core wounds that demand protection from further pain within the armor. They are also your new alarm system. When you feel any of those, you now know there is a need not being met. Awareness is a powerful change agent.

Lao Tzu writes in the *Tao Te Ching* (Tao 78):
>Nothing in the world is softer and weaker than water.
>Yet, it transforms the most rigid of surfaces.
>Nothing can take its place.
>The weak overcomes the strong.
>The soft overcomes the hard.
>Everybody in the world knows this,
>still nobody makes use of it.

Flow is the water energy that transforms the most difficult situations and people. Flow is a power far greater than the mightiest muscle or sharpest sword. Flow requires creativity, intuition, empathy, compassion, courage and the full use of the energy of Love. I think of tenacity when I think of moving bodies of water. A river only subtly changes course when the forces of nature or mankind *force* it to change. As you tenaciously and courageously choose to flow in Love's energy, everything below the river bed, all the limitations and illusions yield.

As water, your feelings are nothing more than a reflection of how you see the situation. No one can *make* you feel anything. Blame, shame, and guilt are a byproduct of plowing through the challenge. The water sees only the topography of the landscape. When you reach the place of flowing, you allow yourself to know when your wound is being touched. This is an optimum space for healing to occur. You empathize with the pain of others and do not take their attacks personally, simply feeling and acknowledging their pain while remaining grounded in your center with your essence of Love. You flow in the path, guided by your intuition, bending, slowing, and flowing in whatever way necessary to reach the other side. In its process, the water often transforms the rigid surfaces it flows over.

There is a balance in living within this space. It does not mean you will always do nice things. Sometimes, you must do the most difficult things, such as walking away or standing firm in your conviction, but you can always do them for Love. You honor the space where you are One with the other person. You seek balance moment by moment, flowing with what life brings you and what that brings up in you.

The moment of surrender is when your energy begins to flow. You no longer have reason to blame others for the hurt they have caused you. You no longer have to hold onto the anger and resentment. Surrender brings a sweetness of acceptance that this is the life you have chosen, consciously or unconsciously, and no matter what has happened in the past, how you move forward is entirely up to you. You have that power. It is not necessarily easy to shift perspective and be willing to see that the person who hurt you is also someone who loves you enough to help you grow. It is not always easy to forgive someone for the hurt that was caused because doing so takes you out of the victim or martyr role and empowers you to move forward. Becoming accountable and moving forward is scary. You can control your limitations. However, surrender opens the channels for the energy of Love to flow freely, which allows you to receive the two most precious gifts, mercy and grace. You need these qualities in order to feel safe enough to step into your authenticity and the infinite field of possibilities.

Just because you surrender and choose to live authentically does not mean life is suddenly a breeze. You are still alive; obviously there are more opportunities to grow within your contract. What it does mean is that you can approach conflict from a very different and open place that creates opportunities to heal on the deepest levels. Though you still have problems to face, you do not have to repeat the same problems. The problems become interesting as you ask, "Ah, what is this? What is below the surface of this issue?" Each layer presents an opportunity. Stay open. Keep digging. And let go.

Conflict Resolution

Challenges and conflicts bring growth, so you are bound to have them throughout your life. Having tools to help you identify, address, and resolve a conflict in the most effective, efficient, and least costly (mentally, physically, and financially) way possible can help minimize the level of conflict and expedite healing. However, a situation can go sideways before you are even aware of it and you are left to wonder what happened. Before you puff out your chest and plow through to prove you are right, take a breath and think through it for a moment.

Identify the situation. What is happening? If your answer is "I don't know" or "That person is being a jerk," this is *not* identifying the situation. Try to step back and do some fact-finding. What is really happening?

First and foremost, do you know the difference between cause and effect in this situation? Often, there are too many variables to have black and white absolutes. Everyone has filters through which they view life. Just like putting on someone else's prescription eyeglasses, you may see through them, but it is rare to have the same vision as another person. What you think is the cause may not be the cause. What someone else is mad about may have little to do with you and more to do with their own hot button that was just pushed. Maybe it was the tone of your voice, the phrasing of your words, or their own insecurities that engaged. Sometimes you will know you have done something wrong and sometimes you will not, just like someone who has pushed your buttons will know sometimes and at other times will not. This is why introspection, objectivity, and clear communication are necessary.

What was *your* role in the emotionally charged situation? I can almost hear it now, "I didn't *do* anything!" This is a common reaction. You're an innocent bystander, right? Think again. All of us make choices *all the time*, consciously and unconsciously. Be brutally honest with yourself about this. You may have pushed a button or pushed the edges a bit more than necessary. Perhaps you're right, you *didn't do* something you said you would do. Maybe you passive aggressively withheld in order to "pay back" for a previous hurt. Here's an example. Your partner wanted something that you did not want so you denied your partner. Or you did meet your partner's desire with reluctance and a poor attitude. Your partner, angry at not having their need met, withholds sex the next time you are feeling amorous. Angry for the cold shoulder, the next time your partner asks for something, you decline as your own payback. So the cycle continues. If there is a conflict, chances are it is not unilateral … fuel, meet fire.

When you are in a direct conflict, name the specific conflict. It is difficult to resolve a conflict when you do not know exactly what the problem is. Far too many people have their buttons pushed and an argument ensues, but what is being argued isn't even really what the problem is about! I think you know what I am talking about here. We have all done it. Or, when an argument begins and suddenly there are additional indiscretions pulled in, and you don't know what you are fighting about. If there is a problem that has an emotional charge, be clear about it. Discuss only that issue. If there are other issues arising, make a commitment to address those next. Stay focused on the task at hand until it is resolved.

Ask, "What specifically did I do that has caused your anger (or whatever appropriate emotion)?" or ask yourself, "What specifically did they do to cause my emotional charge?" As you listen, do so with the heart and body. Where do you feel this emotion in your body? What does it feel like? Do their words resonate as true or does it feel like there is something else? Sometimes, what they are angry about is merely a trigger for something else. Many people hold back because they don't like to hurt others or they have a much deeper fear of abandonment. If it feels to you that there is something else not being said, follow-up with, "Is there anything else?" If there is something more, you can go straight to the roots of that issue. The initial trigger usually masked the roots. No need to waste time on that when there is something deeper to resolve.

As you begin to discuss the problem, become your own mediator. In other words, relinquish your attachments and beliefs around the problem. Listen closely, both to the words and the silence. Observe objectively the facial expressions, body postures, and breathing. Reflect on what you hear and see. Try to understand the other point of view. Breathe slowly and deeply. The extra oxygen will help the muscles remain as relaxed as possible. Seek win-win solutions and implement them.

If you did have a role in what caused the emotional charge, what was your true reason for behaving the way you did or saying what you said? "I don't know" is *not* acceptable. Were you hurt, scared, threatened? Was there a trigger related to a deeper belief or fear within you? Perhaps their words or actions were not ringing true in the energy of Love and you tried to cut through that. It is often hard to watch someone not achieving their full potential and choosing the role of victim. Sometimes our meanness is a way to cut through those limitations. We all have buttons that get pushed. The only way to disconnect the buttons is to figure out what they are wired to and disconnect them.

In conflict, you have two choices: continue the conflict or resolve the conflict. What is the payoff for continuing the conflict? In other words, what benefit is there if you don't address the situation or make any changes? There is *always* a payoff. Always. Maybe it is obvious. You stay in a loveless marriage because you do not want to lose half of your assets. Maybe it is more subtle. You stay in the loveless marriage because you are afraid you'll end up being alone, you'll never find someone else to love you, so the devil you know is better than the one you don't know. Or even more subtle, you stay because it affords you the opportunity to remain a victim, which meets your needs of attention, nurturing, and caring from others outside of the relationship as you share the woes of hardship in your marriage.

We have smaller payoffs every day for the little habits we choose that keep us stuck. You want to lose weight, but you keep eating fast food because it's cheap, convenient, *and* if you lost weight, you'd lose your protective barrier against potential hurt. Sometimes it is difficult and painful to uncover. Once you do, though, you can finally break the habit permanently.

What would you prefer to experience? If you could magically change this situation and no one would get hurt, what would that look and feel like? Do not second-guess. Do not say, "yes, but", just go with it. Let your imagination roam. Really notice how you feel when you go to that place in your imagination. What can you do immediately to increase that feeling in your life? Take action. Ask yourself, "What actions can I take to help me create the ideal situation?" There are many, many options. Sometimes you have to be creative. However, you know doing nothing is going to get you more of the same, so that really isn't an option.

What is your deep-down reason for wanting this preferred experience? For example, I want my mother to be happy and healthy so she can enjoy life to its fullest. Deep down, I want that so she can't make *me* responsible for her happiness because it is a huge amount of pressure and is exhausting. Even typing this, I feel guilty and selfish because I am her only child and she did raise me. That is precisely why we usually want to say, "I don't know," rather than digging down to the true reason. When we courageously step into answering these questions, we can put all the superficial pettiness aside and get to the heart of the matter.

When are you going to take action to move forward? This can be as simple as addressing the unmet needs that caused the behavior in the conflict or it can be a much larger change. Perhaps you are not ready right this moment for a life change. Perhaps you need some time to prepare. That is fine. Take a moment to close your eyes and allow yourself to pretend you are looking at a large calendar. What is the first date your eyes linger on? You have just selected a specific date. Now look at a clock in your mind and notice the time on the clock. That is the specific time in which you will make the change on or by that date. Usually, a date and time will come to mind and you will not have any rational reason for it. Go with it. I think this is part of tapping into our intuition and, like I said earlier, you already have the answers in you!

This happened in a vision quest workshop with one of the participants. I kept getting an intuitive hit that she would make a job change. Without telling her why, I asked her to pick the first date that came to mind, then the time. I told her she would make a significant change in her life by then. Six months later, I received an email saying she had just resigned, and as she was returning to her office after speaking to her boss, something triggered her memory of our class. She took meticulous notes during the workshop, so she flipped back and realized, after the fact, she had made her decision on the date she had chosen during the workshop. Choosing the time and date gives your subconscious something to work with and helps open your conscious mind to see potential you may otherwise overlook.

If you are in a conflict because someone else is engaged in bad behavior, it is time to address the situation. Identify that behavior specifically and clearly. Here is a simple, yet common issue. Let's say cleanliness is important to you and less so to your partner. Dirty clothes are left on the floor in various rooms, dirty dishes are left in the sink for days at a time, and it makes you angry to have to continually pick up after her. The behavior is the disregard for picking up after herself. How does that make you feel? It may help to complete this sentence: "When you do not clean up after yourself, I feel _____." Everyone has some skill at using guilt by putting feelings in needs statements. No one is responsible for your emotions. Therefore, we identify and separate out emotions to bring clarity and take the guilt, shame, and blame out of the equation by basing the situation on facts. Think about why the ideal behavior is important to you. In this example, maybe it's because having a clean home is beautiful and something you have worked hard for, and a clean home feels like a safe space to relax in.

What are your needs that are not being met by this situation? When people see your needs, they are stimulated to help meet those needs from a deeper level, that place of the energy of Love. In our example, your needs are for respect, beauty, and relaxation. Before you make the request for the person to change their behavior, know why you want them to change. Is it for you? Because if it is, they may do it; however, the chances of resentment building is much greater than if they were doing the behavior because *they* wanted to do it. You want her to pick up after herself as an expression of respect because it creates a relaxing space and it honors the beauty of your home. You want her to feel good and respectful about where she lives, too. If, however, cleanliness is not a value she is willing to adopt, you will need to decide if it is something you can continue to live with and, if so, are you willing to pick up after her without resentment because this is *your* value.

Put it all together by stating the behavior, "When you ...," I feel...," and "because I need...." For example, "When you leave your clothes on the floor and dishes lying around, I feel disrespected because we have worked hard for the beauty of our home and this is a space I want to relax in and enjoy." Use your own words, of course.

In clear, positive, action words, request the behavior to change. What do you want the other person to do *exactly*? You could say something like, "I would like you to put your clothes in the hamper when you take them off and put your clean clothes away on the same day they are washed. I would like for you to put your dirty dishes in the dishwasher after you have used them, rather than leaving them in the sink." When you give a request for specific action, there is no confusion around what you really want and no misunderstandings when they follow up by doing what they perceived you were asking.

Ask what needs of your partner are not being met by *not* putting the clothes and dishes away. Maybe she needs to have time to relax and she doesn't want to think about cleaning. Or maybe she hates cleaning and does not have a need for cleanliness. Repeat what you heard her say and ask if you have heard her needs correctly. Ask her to tell you how she heard your needs. Seek ways for how the needs of both parties can be met. Ask your partner if she is willing to do the actions you requested. If she is not, ask what solutions she may have to offer to resolve the unmet needs.

Now, here is the hardest part of it all. Once you go through the entire process, release your expectations of change. Maybe the situation will or will not improve. If it does not, you either have to choose to clean up because this is your need and not hers, or you have to make a more difficult decision of how you want to proceed. However, always recognize and reinforce the behavior you request. When she does what you asked, genuinely thank her. Let her know you recognize and acknowledge her efforts. Build on success and focus on the desired behavior, rather than the undesirable behavior.

To maximize your results, identify and focus on strengths. Know the strengths of others so you can focus on and help increase those strengths. Know and focus on your own strengths. This is also how you learn to trust yourself and others. There is no need to try to force people to engage in activities and tasks that are not their strengths, including yourself. Focusing on the problem will only magnify it so focus on successes. There is no blame. We each have to be accountable for our own actions. Blaming is not going to create solutions to the problems. It just increases negative feelings and allows you to disown your part in the situation. Strengths fuel you and bring you joy. When you are doing something you love, time passes quickly and effortlessly, whereas weaknesses are those things that deplete your energy and make time seem to stand still. You may be great at an activity but still feel drained. Forcing yourself puts you into the fight or flight mode. Give yourself permission to engage the strengths you love and allow everything else to be balanced by the people you bring into your life whose strengths compliment yours. This is a quick and easy way to minimize conflict.

Conflict resolution is not about compromising. I do not believe in compromise. I believe in flexibility. To compromise means to agree by conceding, lessening the value of somebody or something, or exposing somebody or something to danger. Flexibility means to be able to bend without breaking, to adapt to a new situation, and be subject to influence. Can you see how different they are? Flexibility allows space for change and holds the value of both parties in high esteem.

As you become more fluid in your approach to conflict, know that there are reasons why change will not be easy. Remember, for every action there is an equal and opposite reaction. This means that today's problems may have come from yesterday's solutions. Even the absolute best choices in your life could generate other challenges. These problems are simply opportunities to learn and grow. Aim for better balance. As you begin to drive change within you, the system you have created through your thoughts and beliefs will try to hold the course. The harder you push, the harder the system pushes back. Yes, this is the "what you resist will persist" rule. Systems do not take kindly to change. Sit with the resistance and listen to the fears associated. Notice what is below the surface of those fears. Be compassionate with yourself. Send unconditional love to this fear. Allow your heart to absorb the qualities for which it desires. When you hit the wall, so to speak, look for ways to go around the wall or find the cracks in the wall and chip away lovingly there by addressing your needs and the longing in your heart.

Behavior will sometimes grow better before it grows worse. Sometimes the people who love you influence you to change your behavior or perhaps you are pushing someone else to change their behavior. Once the change starts, on the surface it may look like everything is simpatico, while under the surface and in private conversations, grumbling about the change is occurring. Remember, if change is demanded, resentment builds. A person has to *want* to change. Demands cause people to look for the path of least resistance. The easy way out usually leads back in. If easy is not the *best* way, do not do it. It will not work in the long run. For example, dating someone who raises red flags in your mind is compromising. Agreeing to something if it goes against your Truth, ethics, morals, or values just because you do not want an argument or to hurt someone's feelings is compromising. Ignoring bad behavior just because confronting someone might cause conflict is dishonoring your authentic needs. In the long run, sometimes sooner than later, you will revisit the lessons again!

Being authentic requires some vulnerability. True vulnerability keeps us living and growing. Being vulnerable is not about being weak. In fact, it is quite the opposite. It is courageous. It is purely about being open and real. It is about allowing another to see you for who you are in your entirety, including your most sensitive parts where you feel shame. You will always place far more weight on your past than anyone else can. You carry the stories that keep the energy alive. When you open up and embrace the fact that you are perfectly imperfect, you are completely human, and at your core you have the energy of Love, you diffuse the energy of the past. You release so much of the hot buttons and the content around them that conflict simply ceases. When conflicts arise, you know there is something in need of nurturing and healing. True vulnerability is power. Use your power to resolve conflicts and continue your growth.

There is one more important component to conflict resolution. An apology, sincere and when properly used, can transform conflict. However, more often than not, people use it to try to excuse their bad behavior without sincerity. People say "sorry" instead of "pardon me" or "excuse me" when bumping into another person by accident. People apologize to pacify another person. It is as if the purpose of an apology has been forgotten.

There are many ways to deliver an apology. I am a fairly articulate woman, however, my voice is best expressed through writing. Sometimes when you simply cannot speak it, whether the words escape you or the emotions envelope you, simply write your apology. An apology must be sincere. Drop into your heart center for a few minutes to breathe and connect to the goodness and sweetness that resides in you and then express your apology from this space. If you do not feel it, do not say it. It's as simple as that. If you do not understand what you did wrong, figure it out *before* you apologize. Apologizing because you feel you are supposed to will only add fuel to the fire. Humor can be appropriate in an apology *sometimes*. Any good comedian will tell you the importance and value of knowing and reading your audience.

When you apologize, own your responsibility. Leave the "but" out of it. Anything said before the "but" will be forgotten. If you say, "I am sorry, but you started this," your apology might as well have remained unspoken. Express your understanding of why you were wrong and the weight of your mistake. Then offer to make restitution. If this is not possible you can make a sincere offer to behave better as you move forward. If the situation were to arise again, what could be done to avoid escalating the situation to the battle point? You are human. Mistakes will be made as one of the many ways you subconsciously heal your pain or learn to more effectively meet your needs. Saying you'll never do it again is setting yourself up for failure. You can, however, pledge to work on your behavior and ask for help in improving it through communication and positive reinforcements. For example, "When you expressed your anger to me, I understood that I was not present when you needed me. I am so sorry for causing you pain. What can I do to make sure this does not happen in the future? I need you to share with me before it gets to the breaking point. And I need you to support me by pointing out what I am doing right." This is powerful because it is a genuine intention to create change.

Once you have made the apology and communicated your needs, prove your sincerity through actions. In the end, words are meaningless without the backing of actions. Then move on. One apology is enough. If the person is expecting more, something else is alive and that is another matter to work through. Groveling only creates inferiority. That is not equality or efficacy.

Do not apologize for unreasonable expectations. I used to have unbelievably high expectations of myself and others (now they are only high for myself). At the heart of this lies insecurity and the attempt to prove worthiness (or have it proven). Some people expect their significant other to bow to their every need, paying attention only to him/her, and when those expectations are not met, there will be hell to pay, with a new expectation of apologies for everything in order to get back in good grace. No more. Stop. Only own what is yours. If you are dealing with unrealistic expectations, practice the fair fighting techniques in the previous chapter. If those are not working, it is time to move on. Believe me, I am speaking from experience, being alone is much, much better than being together and miserable. If you have stated your needs clearly and shared your beliefs as compassionately as possible, avoiding attacks, then you do not need to apologize if the other person remains angry. Likely, there is something much deeper than the surface issue at hand. You have the choice to let it rest or try to understand and take on that deeper issue. It is your choice.

An apology is a commitment towards healing both yourself and the recipient. It takes courage to be honest and transparent and to risk being judged or not forgiven. Even if things do not work out the way you expect them to, they will always work out the way they need to for the sacred contract. Use the situation to uncover more layers of remaining hurt rather than cycling back into victim mode and adding layers. Act with integrity and surrender the need to be right or in control in order to let your energy of Love flow freely.

Acceptance

Acceptance might be one of the hardest qualities for a human being to embrace. There is an inner child within all of us that is awakened when our tender spots are touched. Our inner child wants what it wants and no amount of reasoning is going to change that. The only way to deal with that frustration and pain is to send love to the tender spots, to the inner child, to the fear that is simply trying to protect you from pain. Ah, yes, that old pain again. "Okay," you say, "Bring it." When you choose to sit with it, listen to it, and send it love, acceptance comes, almost effortlessly. Acceptance allows you to stop taking things personally. Instead of the "What if's" you ask, "So what if?" So what if she isn't doing what you want? So what if he doesn't call you back, if he doesn't follow through, if your expectations are not met? One of my closest friends taught me a valuable lesson when he said, most lovingly, "Wendy, what other people think of you is none of your damn business." Acceptance of the facts, wihtout emotional attachment and storytelling, is a powerful tool: fluid, courageous, and strong. Transformative.

Western culture has created a duality around happiness. On one end of the spectrum is the expectation that happiness is good and everyone should be happy. On the other end are the overwhelming messages that happiness comes from outside of you with the subtle message that you need something else to make you happy. That is the purpose behind most advertising; you need to buy their product in order to be better and then you will be happy. How can you ever *have* enough in order to *be enough* to attain happiness? That feels hopeless and is precisely why advertising works so well. If you allow someone else to define happiness and what will make you happy, happiness will remain elusive. When happiness is outside of you, the message is that light emotions (joy, love, happiness, peace) are good and the shadow emotions (fear, anger, sadness) are bad. The duality of good and bad is limiting.

Remember, what you resist will persist. If you are continually repressing the shadow emotions and struggling to grow the light emotions, you are living in fight or flight mode because you are fighting off a part of YOU. We have already discussed what that will do to your body. You were created with all emotions inside of you. There is room for *all* emotions. Rather than resisting the shadows, embrace them. Use them as a guide to learn for what your heart is thirsting. Accept them as a part of you. You choose to come into this life to grow and experience some spiritual qualities more fully. In order to do that, you have to allow yourself to feel all emotions. You are everything.

On the journey to acceptance, maintain what the Buddhists call a beginner's mind. Just like a child learning, there is curiosity and openness for new concepts. The duality of right and wrong closes off options. A beginner's mind keeps the options open. John Paul Lederach coined the term "paradoxical curiosity" in *The Moral Imagination: The Art and Soul of Building Peace* as, "abiding respect for complexity, a refusal to fall prey to the pressures of dualistic categories of truth, and inquisitiveness about what may hold seemingly contradictory social energies in a greater whole." Ignorance and duality are limiting. Knowledge is expansive and empowering when used to explore and grow. As you increase knowledge, new attitudes are employed that eventually develop into beliefs. These beliefs support specific behaviors that benefit not only you but the collective community. Just as a curious child learns, you gain knowledge through the constant and yet illusive search for "why."

You cannot change the past. You can, however, stop lying, running from it and accept responsibility for *your* part. History is alive. You carry it with you on a cellular level. Your soul longs to live truthfully and authentically. Though you do not know your future, you can certainly create a desired vision. The present is about beginnings. Take the best of what you know and evolve into the person you want to be. Your strength and power to do this comes from being vulnerable enough to take risks needed to build a future. This beginning is an impregnation of authenticity, transparency, honesty, and the energy of love. The birth is a surrendering to your soul. Your heart will be cracked open to the vastness of all that you are, creating recognition of the energy of Love in all beings. Your soul will dance again, silly and child-like, blissfully connected to the Universal Love. There is nothing to control and nothing beyond "I Am." As you accept that you are everything and nothing, you open up to experience everything because of the interconnectedness flowing through Love's energy in all. Expansive and amazing quite understate that feeling.

You have lived with a set of beliefs that have served to protect you and thus, have masked your authenticity for too long. These have been unexamined because they are so deeply subconscious. I am challenging them in you right now. Rise up and start the process of self-awareness and acceptance. Reflect on your past and visualize what you want in your future. Repeat this self-inquiry and self-study so that it becomes second nature. Let yourself feel the depth of knowing that you are fully supported. There are many layers that you will continue to uncover. Accept this as a process. You can choose to view the process as a nuisance or you can pretend you are an explorer and view it as an adventure of discovery.

Be done with the status quo. This is not to say that you are not allowed to want the finer things in life. The difference now is knowing you do not *need* them and they will not make you happier (or happy, for that matter). Now, your joy comes from the exchange of the energy of Love. You understand and can experience the joy of the little things in life that is all around you and in you. A smile from someone you care for is priceless. A hug at the right moment can fuel you. Laughter is a valuable currency. So is silence. In the silence, you can hear and feel the love, strength, courage, and peace that drive you forward or keeps you in place. You can literally feel the energy of Love in everything.

With an open heart, you can recognize, honor, and respect the oneness and interconnectedness of all. Moreover, you respect life and death, placing equal value on both. This is important because, when you understand death, you understand the value of life and the intricacies of the experience. Understanding the permanence of death of the form we are in now provides the springboard of knowledge into the depth of knowing that wishing away life, wasting time, and not stepping fully into your purpose is unacceptable. Create a culture around you that values and promotes awareness and compassionate inquiry. In committing to this level of living, you are also embracing and living in a space of openness, transparency, and integrity.

Acceptance is the big leap that takes you from victim to an empowered, Divine, infinite being. You are powerful. When you take responsibility for your feelings, needs, and actions, you accept and embrace that power. You have both light and shadow emotions. They are neither good nor bad, simply energy that can serve as an amazing guide. When you recognize that we are all Divine, infinite beings here on this life journey in order to experience all emotions (or Divine qualities) more fully, you accept that we are simply playing out our sacred contracts. There is no more need for shame, blame, guilt, or useless fear. When you accept that you came to this life with a unique expression of the energy of Love, you know you have a gift that this world needs right now or you wouldn't be here. Acceptance allows you to start using that gift rather than playing small or being a victim. You will make an impact on *your* world, whether that is one person or five billion people. Accept that everything up to this point has been an opportunity for you to experience, heal, and grow. Accept that

YOU are so much more than you have allowed yourself to believe up until this moment. Believe it. The world needs the authentic version of you now.

Vision Quest

There is expansiveness beyond the borders of your mind. As a child, you could imagine anything. You could transport yourself to other places, be someone else, live other lives, all from the confines of a bedroom or playground. I grew up with a park across from my house. In the park was a concrete picnic table. That table served as a house, castle, school, hospital, NASA control station, a kitchen (mud pies), a shop, and the White House. The world was whatever I wanted it to be. What is it about becoming an adult that hinders the imaginative creativity and curious wonder? The only limitation holding you back right now *is* your mind.

You can use your imagination to springboard beyond the perceived borders of limitations. Imagination is the vehicle to the expansiveness where you live authentically. Go beyond your wildest dreams. The key to success is leveraging your mind, your experiences, your time, and your money in that exact order! Paulo Coehelo writes in *The Alchemist*, "When you want something with all your heart, the Universe will conspire to make it happen." Whether it is the Universe conspiring or just your subconscious mind following the mental maps and models YOU create, you will get exactly what you are most deeply, subconsciously thinking, feeling and believing. That is why it is so important to get crystal clear about what you want, what you believe, and what you feel. Your imagination can catapult you into something even greater than you are capable of imagining.

You have internalized the events of your life and created a story of your life. Where are you now in your story? Do you feel like you have been the author or simply a character that others have created? What is your role in your life, with your tribe, in the world? Most of my clients have no idea what their part is in their own story, let alone the bigger, collective story. So many people go through life not knowing their purpose for being alive. By the time you are done with this section, you will have a clearer vision.

No matter how boring, ordinary, or mundane you think your life is, everyone has the right to live an epic story. Epic is so subjective. For some, that could mean aiming to start a massive, history changing movement or experiencing one great, fearless adventure after another. For others, epic is about being the best version of their self- a great friend, partner, and/or parent. Choosing to live an epic story does not mean that you ignore, forget, or even change your past. In order to live epically, you simply have to reframe your relationship to your past. YOU, my friend, have the power to narrate the meaning of your life.

You already know your history. After all, you survived it. Let's look a little deeper from a different perspective. Put on your detective hat because it is time to go searching and exploring. You are simply fact-finding. If something comes up that is in need of healing, I recommend either stopping and addressing or temporarily setting it aside. As you look at your past, particularly if you have painful stories, it is easy to become emotionally charged. If that happens, ask your heart what it desires in that moment and allow yourself to receive it, then continue on the fact-finding mission. If the charge is persistent, go back and do some exploration and healing and return when you are ready. Have fun with this process. Risk being willing to be surprised at what you find, too. Let the mission begin.

Where did you come from? This is far deeper than where were you born and raised, although that has its importance. This is also about who raised you, who was around when you were growing up, and what/who influenced you. What was your family life like? We tend to imitate those adults who make an impression on us. In hindsight you will see those adults as they really were, not as your childlike wonder created them. Understanding that, you can often identify commonalities of your patterns with the adults you were raised around. Knowing what you know now, you can also see their woundedness and how that played a role in their behavior without judging, blaming, or condoning that behavior.

What was your community like? What were the overwhelming values shared in the community? Was your family aligned with those values or were you in some way an outsider? These are important aspects influencing your growth (or lack of). If there was something you were missing that your community didn't provide, you might to fill the emptiness by giving of yourself to the point of a fault or declining into a dark hole of entitlement.

What was your personality as a kid? What did you love to do? Were there things that you were discouraged from doing that you loved? What did you long to have that seemed illusive? Did you feel like you were chasing love and adoration? Even if you knew your family always loved and adored you, as have most of your friends and partners, was there something that felt illusive in all of it? Who influenced you?

You may be starting to see a pattern emerge from your childhood. If you wanted to get really deep with this you could break it down into different ages and explore deeper, though a big picture and the general facts are all that is necessary. What came up as you looked back at your childhood? How did it feel? Was it easy or difficult? What three words would best describe your childhood? If you could change those three words to more ideal words, what would you chose? Remember those three words. We will be using them again shortly. Moving on, let's explore the influences on your adult life.

What do you share in common with others who are important to you? You attract people to you whose thoughts are in sync with the vibration of your thoughts and beliefs. The people you most admire in a historical context may be completely different than the people with whom you surround yourself. Take a moment to look at both. If you admire a historical figure, what qualities do you most admire? What qualities do you share in common? What qualities do you admire and not share? Of those people that you open up to and share your life with, what qualities do they have in common with you? What qualities of theirs do you admire and not share? How can you increase these desirable qualities in your life right now? This is an excellent question for brainstorming, particularly if you invite your inner child to play along in the session.

What are the best and worst moments in your life? These tend to be the stories you tell and re-tell, allowing them to define you. This time, state it simply as a fact, without the emotional attachment to them. What was that one really awful moment as a child or adolescent that caused you to be more cautious with your authenticity? An interesting side exploration is to take that moment and go through some of the exercises in chapter 7. When have you felt most alive? What were you doing? Who was there? This question can be really hard for people who have been living an inauthentic life for a long time. I think the most alive I ever felt was stepping into a river in Nepal to bathe and ride the elephants. There is a photo of me doing this and I have had people who barely knew me ask for a copy because it is so obvious the extreme joy and pure bliss that I felt at that moment. I feel alive when I catch and surf a wave. It doesn't matter if it is only for four seconds. For me, I am completely present for four seconds- just me, the board and the ocean playing together.

What turns on your inner geek? These are the things that excite you and make you feel as if time stands still. So often, people give these things up when they are in a time of struggle or survival mode. These are the very things you need in order to refresh, renew, and re-establish balance. Is it any wonder that if you struggle to know what you are passionate about and what engages your mind that you would complain of feeling unbalanced, ungrounded or off-center? Pay attention the next time you are in that state.

What's your biggest fear? Be honest with this. People like to think they are fearless. We are human, therefore, we have fears. For me, it is reaching the end of my life and finding that I wasted so many opportunities to love and make a difference. What would happen if your biggest fear came true? Would it stop you from trying again? A lot of my clients are afraid of people seeing their "real" self and no longer liking them. I ask them, "If your friends saw your authenticity, would they stop being your friends?" For the most part, the answer is no. If someone ends a relationship with you when you step into your authenticity, the person is doing you a huge favor because they aren't really your friend anyway. Would your family stop loving you if you were unapologetically authentic? Ultimately, no, they would not. They may be hurt and their pride may cause them to end the relationship, though they never stop loving you, regardless of what they may say. Perhaps ending the relationship is a gift in itself because it liberates you to be you. Would you lose your job, your home, your life? It is rare that you lose your life for living authentically. Unfortunately, there is still too much prejudice, righteousness, and bigotry in the world. Many great leaders have lost their life for speaking their Truth. It happens. You, fortunately, have a greater chance of losing your life by falling down the stairs. However, I hope you live epically, healthfully, and authentically for a long time.

All the questions you answered so far shaped how you got to where you are now. The next set identifies how you presently interact, think, and believe. This is going to take you a little while to answer. *Please* do not rush through these. Give yourself permission to feel them with your heart as well as think about them. Ask your closest friends and relatives for some input if you get stuck.

What makes you smile? (Activities, people, events, hobbies, projects, etc.) What three words did you use to describe your ideal childhood? What do you do now to increase those feelings in your life? What were your favorite things to do in the past: as a child, a teenager, and a young adult? What about now? What activities make you lose track of time?

What makes you feel great about yourself? Who inspires you? This can be anyone you know or do not know, alive or dead. Family, friends, authors, artists, and leaders are prime examples. These are the people who have helped shape your thoughts, beliefs, values, and desires. What qualities inspire you in each person listed above? What are three to six of your deepest values? Who are/were your mentors? What causes do you strongly believe in? Connect with? What injustices make you angry? What topics get you on a proverbial soapbox?

What are you naturally good? (Skills, abilities, gifts.) What do people typically ask you for help with? If you had to teach something, what would you teach and to whom? If you could get a message across to a large group of people, who would those people be? What would your message be? Given your talents, passions and values, how could you use these resources to serve, to help, to contribute to others?

What would you regret not fully doing, being or having in your life? What were some challenges, difficulties, and hardships that you've overcome or are in the process of overcoming? How did you do it? What is your purpose?

The last question has to allow energy, be that money or resources, to flow through you effortlessly for the greater good of others. As you awaken and reconnect to your energy of Love, you will help others help themselves or help others who cannot help themselves. Ambition originated in the mind will attract material possessions, titles, and many other things at any cost. Ambition that originates from the heart, however, is pure. It has no need for competition. Rather than harming, it is healing and serving to the individual with heartfelt ambition as much as it heals and serves others. That is an energy that attracts exactly what is desired in your heart.

It is time to start thinking about what you want your life to become when you are living authentically, aiming for the highest version of yourself. This is your "ideal life." So it's time to dream bigger than the biggest galaxy. This is the mind blowing, how-is-that-even-possible kind of dreaming that sends a real, clear message to the Universe and to the recesses of your mind to update those maps. Sure, you can dream about the superficial stuff like toys and beautiful playmates, financial limitlessness and more. I want to challenge you to go beyond that. This is the life that your essence is calling out to live.

Imagine that I am waving my magic, silver wand that lights up and makes a brrrrrriiiiinnnggg sound over your beautiful head. The glittering fairy dust falls down over you and suddenly everything changes. You have no more obstacles. Money, resources, a lack of knowledge are not an issue. All of the limitations in your past or present... gone! In this magical space, you see the life your *heart* desires. I have gathered all the elements (earth, fire, water, air, ether), the highest version of you, and the energy of Love to help you with this process. There is nothing left to fear. Now what?

Take a few minutes. Set a timer for 10 minutes and imagine you are waking up in your ideal life. Drink in the details as you move through the day and into the night until eventually you're crawling back into bed, reflecting on and appreciating the day. When the timer sounds, answer the following questions. What was your life like? Who was in it? Where were you? What did you do with your time? Where did you live? Describe your living situation in as much detail as possible. Were you in a relationship/partnership? Describe it. What qualities does your partner possess? What activities do they enjoy doing? How did you feel? How did you cover your living expenses? What was your health status? How do you stay healthy? Details. How spiritually connected were you? What do you do to maintain and grow that connection? How did you stay intellectually engaged? How did you grow as a person? What did you love the most about it? How did you play? What made you feel appreciated? Loved? How did you define success? Why? How would you know when you have attained success? What would the ideal life feel like?

Now, go back and read what you wrote. Write it as a story. Paint a picture with words, starting with, "In my ideal life….." Once you have completed that, ask yourself, "Does this vibrate what is most deeply desired in me? Does it awaken the energy of Love that I want to carry forward and project into the world?" If it does not make you feel more expanded, lighter, more alive, go back and revise until it does. This is YOUR life, not anyone else's. Your answers do not need to be rational or make sense. They just need to *feel* right.

You may have dreamt big here and this ideal life may *seem* impossible and scary. That is great! Keep it as it is. Usually, people do not dream big enough when they do this exercise because they are still trapped believing they are not worthy of such an epic life. I know the first few years (not times, but *years*) that I did this, I held back. Each time I did the exercise, I could reflect back and see how the most impossible things, even though I was holding back, were coming true from previous iterations. So the next time I pushed my edges a little more. Now, I just go for it. Why not? It is my life, my epic story. I only get one shot. I would rather hit the stars while reaching for the moon than stay grounded on Earth, worrying and regretting.

Take your final story and break it down to the most important things in the following categories, writing one general sentence to describe each of the following categories of your ideal life: relationships, health, finances, intellectual, emotional, spiritual, career, home, travel, lifestyle, values, and family.

Use this information to create a vision board. Cut out images and words that reflect your ideal life. Put this somewhere you can see it everyday. Re-create the board using the same exercise each year. Some things will remain because they take a little more time to come to fruition. However, you will be shocked at how many things on your vision board happen in just one year! By looking at it daily, you are reinforcing the new maps that you are creating. Your brain can analyze options and send you a guiding emotion that will direct you closer to your vision by helping you make the right choices to stay on target. Sometimes that requires saying no to an alluring offer because your gut is telling you that choice will take you away from your dreams.

Everyday, look at your board and *really* feel, with gratitude as if it has already happened, envision what it would feel like if you were living that life. When you have to make decisions, ask yourself if your decision is in alignment with the vision and if not, revise it. Take small steps every day to elevate your vibrational frequency and get closer to the vision. Imagining without action is rather pointless. Release your attachment to the outcome; you simply do not know how exactly this ideal will be delivered to you. You planted the seeds, you raised your energy, now it is time to be present, take the action, and let the energies you desire be drawn to you.

We are not done yet. You need to narrow your list down to the top five priorities that you will focus on over the next year. To narrow it, you are going to have to feel with your gut rather than think with your head. There is no second-guessing here and the process needs to be speedy. This is a bit like speed dating meets March Madness. Go with your initial response. You can do this with a friend or you can simply imagine a person you highly respect sitting in front of you, holding your list. They are going to go through the process of making you choose. Again, DO NOT THINK! Use your gut. If you hesitate in answering, imagine them *yelling* the choices at you. Answer quickly.

Using some of the categories of your ideal life (relationship/family, health, finances, intellectual, spiritual, career, home, and travel), choose one or two words to sum up what you identified previously. Here is an example list:

Relationship/family- ideal partner

Health- pain free

Finances- millionaire

Intellectual- read a book a week

Spiritual- meditate daily with ease

Career- helping millions

Home- beach house

Travel- yes, please!

Relationships
(ideal partner)

Health
(pain free)

pain free

Financial
(millionaire)

Intellectual
(read a book a week)

millionaire

pain free

Spiritual
(mediate daily with
ease)

Career
(helping millions)

helping
millions

Home
(Craftsman
bungalow on a
beach

helping
millions

Travel
(yes please)

travel

pain free

Pain free was my #1 and helping millions was my #2 priority.
Travel and millionaire would then compete for #3 and #4. Then I
would take home, spiritual, intellectual, and relationship through

the process to determine #5. Ninety percent of the time when I do this exercise in workshops or with clients they are shocked at what their true priority is. Often, the ego tries to protect and pushes you toward what you "should" want rather than what your soul desires. When done correctly, this exercise takes the ego out and allows the soul to guide. While healing my injury was a priority at that time, money and career were my focus. My soul knew that the injury would hold all of that back. This exercise allowed me to refocus and I am forever thankful. What the doctors said as impossible was incorrect and as of this writing, I am 97% healed. That has made all the difference in the world, my career, relationships, soul, and me.

Create a scorecard. How will you know when you have successfully completed or attained these items? What will be different from now? Write two or three things that will help you recognize when you have reached your goals. For example, "I will know I am pain free when I can run without noticing my back and hip, when I can do a forward fold or plow in yoga, when I can sit crossed legged again." Do this for each item on your list.

Go through each of the five and think of three things you will need to do to reach each goal. Every week, make it a priority to do at least one thing daily from this list of 15 action items. Write each goal and your three action items on sticky notes or note cards and leave them in places you will see them regularly. These are the gentle reminders to help your brain rework the maps.

Now you have a solid foundation for your dream. Think about your ideal life and ask yourself these questions: What will change when I am in my ideal life? How will I be different than I am now? What will I do differently? Who will be in my life? Where will my epic story play out? How will this ideal life really feel?

Remember, what you choose to focus on is exactly what you will receive in abundance. When you engage in behaviors and participate in activities that expand you, you are co-creating and reinforcing positive emotions. These are better than any drug and have no negative side effects. Every morning, write three things you can do today that will bring you more joy. This is about expanding your pleasure. When you disconnected from the energy of Love, it was due to pain. Subconsciously you became aware that it was not okay to feel good. It is time to give yourself permission to re-experience pleasure on every level. I highly recommend creating a pleasure list of 50-500 items. They need to vary from big to small. Included on this list will be the things you think may give you pleasure but you have not experienced yet, the things you know give you pleasure, and perhaps some old favorites that you have stopped doing.

If you don't know where to start, here are some examples from my list and the lists of some of my clients:

Race car driving, bubble baths, sex in the shower, eat my way through Italy, go to a Spring Training game in the middle of the week, own a Mercedes SL63, live in Chicago, have sex in public, see the aurora borealis, be fed chocolate-covered strawberries in bed, see Paris in the spring, find my partner's panties with a sexy note in my messenger bag, run a half marathon, read a book in a hammock one afternoon, hook up with a cute redhead, spontaneous day trips, live music, have a housecleaner, skydiving, hugs, home cooked meals, receive flowers, little notes from my partner, weekly happy hour with my friends, alone time, massages, pedicures, watching a dog roll in the grass or play with other dogs, mountain bike ride in the middle of the day on an empty trail, ride the train cross-country, a day off work for no reason with no agenda or plan, having the time to get a tan, rent a RV and drive to a National Park and just be there, learn to fly fish, ride a motorcycle on a nice day with no to-do list, play catch with my dog, a glass of my favorite beer, the smell of the ocean, feeling a naked body next to mine, a back scratch, the smile from eating something new that totally rocks, being successful on a project, paying off debt, the smell of hiking in the desert after a rain, leave work early to watch a movie and enjoy buttered popcorn with butter on bottom, middle, and top.

I think you get the idea. Feel free to borrow any of those. We certainly do not own the rights to them and, if they make you happier, then the whole world will benefit! Put your list where others can see it. Of course, use discretion if necessary. You will be surprised because when people know that you like something, they will try to make it happen.

When you become grateful for what you have now and all you will have (that big, wild, ideal life of yours), you become a magnet for more. Oh, yes! Please and thank you very much! What are you grateful for in your life? What do you appreciate? Nothing is too big or too small. I am grateful for my toenails, my miraculous body with the heart that pumps and the lungs that intake oxygen and expire carbon dioxide along with all the parts that work and are strong and healthy, for my friends and family, my home and garden, my gifts. Try to think of five things every day that you are grateful for in your life. I start my day with this process and include what I have and what I want, saying it as if it is already true. The days I practice this seem to be so much better than the days I forget.

You *will* get exactly what you want. Just remember, sometimes it is not quite in the package you expected. When I moved to Arizona, I wanted to create healing gardens for chronically and terminally ill patients. I wanted them to benefit from the healing power of plants and receive the soothed by their beauty. I became a yoga instructor instead. Now, I help the dis-eased and those with chronic pain, weight issues, and the traumas that cultivate his or her inner, emotional garden. Ultimately, I got what I wanted. I just never expected it to come in this package!

You have completed this vision quest. Be open. Be present. Stay focused. You have your vision, *now go for it*. You *do* deserve this magnificent, wild, succulent, radical, juicy life you dreamed up… and so much more!

Creating a new story

Now you are aware of having a sacred contract that is driven by your desire to experience the Divine qualities more fully. You have separated yourself from the energy of Love to feel the shadow qualities more deeply. You created stories that made sense of pain and beliefs. Going through this process helped you survive. Good job. I don't say that sarcastically. It is great because if you can create those stories and beliefs, guess what- you can create new stories and beliefs based on facts and truth.

You have begun the long journey Home from the dark night of your soul. No one knows the experiences you have survived. Though some may know of those experiences, no one knows the challenge, pain, fear, or depth of all emotions, except you. Those who were with you in this sacred contract have experienced each and every moment through their own perception of reality. People have not loved you in the way you know Love from the place of Home and it hurts. In the absence of Love's flow, it has seemed far easier to build armor and *pretend* to live within society "normally," going through the motions and repeating like a sacred mantra, "I'm fine." Unfortunately, that is a slow, dull and painful death. It is a self-imposed prison with no walls, only a gate, which is not locked. That armor only protects your pain. It limits the flow. It is time to surrender into your authenticity.

What does it mean for you to be yourself? What have you hidden out of fear of judgment or rejection? Of course you have the freedom to keep hiding. Just know that you are fighting your authenticity and fleeing in fear. Every day you experience the fight or flight mode. Your body is paying the price, whether you are aware of it at this moment or not. Allow yourself to dream for a bit about what life would be like if you were to be fully you. Risk being surprised. Allow yourself to see the positive outcomes and the scary outcomes. What would change? What are the consequences of that change? What is the fear below the surface surrounding the consequences? What is even deeper than that?

Look, being fully you may mean walking away from security into the unknown. It may mean losing relationships, leaving a career, or moving. That is scary. The unknown can paralyze you. If it were easy, everyone would be doing it. Being authentic is a risk that carries the potential for great loss or great rewards. In this case, it has the potential for both. You should know, though, that everyone I have met that has taken the risk of being their authentic self has had no regrets, despite any losses along the way.

Who are you? As explained previously, at your core, you are the energy of Love. You are sohum. How do you express that energy of Love? You learn this the same way you learn about a new love interest or friend. You ask questions, you listen, you do new things, you explore new ideas, most of all, you open up to exploring and are willing to be surprised by what you discover. Welcome to the great adventure. It will take a lifetime to learn everything there is to know about yourself because you are infinite and a lifetime just might not be long enough. Listen to your heart and allow yourself the opportunity to receive the qualities your heart desires from the Divine. Use your new communication skills to express your needs and desires, "I feel... and I need." Then allow yourself to receive it. There is nothing wrong with being open to being fully authentic and having no clue how to live it. The how is not really that important. All that is required of you is to be open and willing to take small steps.

You have worth. Knowing that truth (even if you still struggle to believe it) means you are important, have value, and hold a special place in this world because you have something to contribute. You are here in this life right now because you are needed. Your gifts are needed. Yes, YOU! You *are* enough, always have been and always will be. Keep recognizing this, realizing this, and touching the sweetness of that "enoughness." This is where confidence builds. This is where your beliefs begin to shift and convictions take root. Seek to understand what your closest friends love most about you and how they view your best qualities. They do not view you from the faulty belief system that you view yourself, so they have insight into your truth. Take that information and build on it.

Being authentic is not arrogant or egotistical. Being authentic provides humility because there is a recognition that we are all the same at our essence. When the energy of Love is flowing, as well as when you are engaged in a component of a sacred contract, you are receiving a precious gift. The recognition of that is humility. You know the preciousness and can cherish it. When you are in an ego state, you engage the victim persona or you try to use your power to manipulate. Either way, you are not connected to the Love. Humility allows you to receive Love and to have your needs met without expectations that fuels the energy of Love. I say, "Yes! Bring it!"

Allow your joy to come from the exchange of the energy of Love with others. Eric Greitens tells in his book, *The Heart and the Fist*, of advice he received during BUD/S training to become a Navy SEAL. "If you're a real frogman (SEAL), then every time a woman leaves your side, she'll feel better about herself." What if you treated *everyone* you came in contact with that way? You don't even have to say a word to them, simply smile with the intention that their life be more wonderful in the moment and beyond. Just imagine, a whole world full of people that would treat *every single person* they came in contact with *every single moment* of *every single day* with the same love, compassion, dignity, and respect that you wish to receive yourself.

Allow yourself to experience the joy of the little things, of the life that is all around you and in you. In the silence, you can hear and feel the love, strength, courage, and peace that drives you forward or keeps you in place. The soul wants to be known completely, wants to feel all its power come to fruition and dance with the weak spots that need love. The soul wants creativity, sensuality, passion, purpose, generosity, and tenderness with which to teach the fearful, controlling, angry, needy parts of you. The rigid ego fears the unknown and fights mightily, trying to define these facets as good or bad. They are, quite frankly, neither! The ego also tries to throw up the red flags to warn you of the danger of approaching the boundaries of safety and security, those very subconscious agreements that share "always" and "never." These red flags are reminders of the tender places longing for love, compassion, understanding, and acceptance. The soul wants to shatter the protective armor around your heart while the ego desperately builds and repairs the armor. Which will you choose to listen to from now on?

How do you discover and live the Divine qualities? First and foremost, open your heart to receiving them. Then, seek them in everything. Every living being has that shared essence. Everything made has been touched by someone with that essence. Honoring that essence does not make you weak or soft. In fact, it is quite the opposite. It is the ultimate power recognizing sohum or "I Am That." You become aware that you are both creator and destroyer. You have the power to lift up, heal, bring joy, manifest, or the power to shut it all down.

There is a cycle of balance; life and death, creation and destruction. We need balance. We are wise to release duality of defining them as good or bad. Just because you do not understand why something has been created or destroyed, just because it may hurt or feel good, does not make it good or bad, it simply exists. Every thing that hurts or challenges is an opportunity to grow and heal. Everything. Even the most unexplainable. Everything provides you an opportunity to practice gratitude, a magnetic quality that conveys honor and respect to Love. There is a South

African word, Ubuntu, which roughly means, "I am you and you are I." Everything good that happens to you happens to me. Everything challenging that happens to you happens to me. You are your brother's keeper, so to speak. Interconnected. The survival of society depends on the level of health within the interconnectedness and the relationships that develop within the circles of influence. Knowledge of history allows you to pursue a future that is built upon the strength of interconnectedness. Knowledge of Love allows you live and help others live authentically.

What makes you feel alive? Your purpose may or may not have anything to do with changing the world. Perhaps it is providing a loving, supportive environment that allows others to receive love and nurturing that allows them to more fully express themselves authentically. Perhaps it is educating. Perhaps it is standing up to injustice. Maybe it is creative expression. Creating your new story requires being open to living your purpose and passion. The things that bother you are the very things you have the ability to bring healing energy to through your Love. The things that fuel you and make you lose track of time are the very things that make life worth living, which creates confidence, self-trust, and worth in yourself and others. There is no longer a need for you to fear living your purpose. The energy of Love is in you, flows through you, and expands out of your body through this purpose. There is no longer a need to hide your passions. The need to shrink or be *less than* no longer serves you. It is time! Allow the being you are, all the Love, intelligence, and energy come fully alive. Surrender into all that is in you that is ready to be birthed. The experience of living your purpose and your passions are waiting for you. Will you say, "Yes!"?

By saying, "yes," you are also opening to vulnerability. Every single person in this world has the ability to experience every single emotion in its entirety. Everyone has fear and courage, joy and pain, anger and calmness. Vulnerability means opening up to someone and asking them to accept you for who you are and yet, you have been so afraid of being seen and hurt that you don't show the real you. Are you going to be judged? Sure. Few people know how to live in a place of non-duality and loving unconditionally. Besides, judgment is simply a reminder that limitations are present, either ours or someone else's. Limitations require harmonizing. Congratulations, being judged just became a gifted tool for you. Will you be hurt? Sure. It is simply an opportunity to recognize that you expected someone else to meet your need when inside of you is the very energy that can meet those needs. When you are willing to meet those needs by surrendering into that Divine Love, you open the space to look at the essence of others and love them unconditionally. When you are willing to see others as perfectly perfect Divine beings having a human experience, trying to feel the Divine qualities fully, both shadow and light aspects, then you can engage intimacy. Even when the energy of Love is temporarily disconnected, you know where to tap into the source. You can always return, fill your heart, and practice forgiving yourself and others, and meeting your needs. That is healing. Reconnecting and re-membering is the point of intimacy.

When you allow yourself to be open to Love energy, you experience sensuality. Engage all the senses. There is so much to experience. Slow down to see, hear, smell, taste and touch. This is a deep connection. Sensuality is the physical expression of intimacy, particularly in intimate communion with the Divine. What if you *could* be the eyes, ears, nose, tongue, and nerve endings of the Divine? Would you stop to smell a rose or inhale a bit deeper when you pass the bakery baking bread? Would you take your time to taste the home cooked meal? Would you be less inclined to ingest anything processed? Would you chose to listen to silence or beautiful music rather than the evening news? Would you hug more fully to feel the heartbeat and breath of the other person? Would you let your eyes linger over beauty? What if you allowed the Divine to experience physical activity or sex through your body? This is how the ordinary moments of life become quite extraordinary and life becomes an amazing adventure!

Living authentically expands gratitude. When you are grateful, you want to share all that juiciness. When you tap into that unconditional love it feels so radically amazing that you want to fill the world with it. The brilliance of that is that it is possible because the energy of Love is in *everyone*. How can you share your Love unconditionally? This isn't about giving up all your worldly possessions and living a monastic existence. On the contrary, this is about finding your balance that you meet your needs, you express your Love, you live your purpose and passion and you hold space for others to do the same. It's about generously seeking the essence in another, honoring their light, even when their actions do not best express their light. It is about helping those who do not know yet or cannot help themselves. It is about being generous with your responsibility and accountability with your thoughts, words and actions, with your compassion to self and other, with all your emotions knowing that there is room for the shadow and light of all of them.

Are you willing to live honestly and transparently? You no longer have to be anything you are not. You no longer have to agree with something you do not agree with out of fear of being left or judged. The time has come to speak your truth compassionately, to live your convictions. You have begun to explore your beliefs and started creating new beliefs. There is a quote by John Ruskin hanging on the wall of Sevagram, Gandhi's last home, that reads, "The essence of lying is in deception, not in words; a lie may be told by silence, by equivocation, by the accent on a syllable, by the glance of the eye attaching a peculiar significance to a sentence; and all these kinds of lies are worse and baser by many degrees than a lie plainly worded."

When I read this quote, I understood that lying by omission is equally as traumatizing and unjust as lying outright. Both are based on intention, though none are on a conscious or soul level; they are an ego-driven action to protect from hurt or to validate the deep seeded beliefs of faulty mental models. Are you willing to be honest with yourself? You are the only thing that has separated you from the flow of Love's energy. Everything that is heavy, angry, painful, frustrating, disappointing, constricting, everything that has been abusive and you have wanted to run from, has been your choice to hold onto. Be honest. Now you know the shadow qualities, are you ready to re-experience the Light? If you are willing to drop all the old stories, if you are willing to just be you, you will not need to attract the people and situations that keep you recycling the lessons to meet the unmet needs. Knowing how to let go is not important, simply saying, "yes" allows that energy of Love to do what it needs to do in you. The fear of being judged if you're you is irrelevant now. Everything that is not serving you will be removed. Its purpose is done. In your transparency, you gain clarity.

In your authenticity, you live honorably with integrity. You may be able to fool everyone else. You cannot hide from yourself, though. When you take 100% responsibility for your thoughts, words, and actions, that is the highest form of integrity. To deny your part in this life is dishonorable and breaks your ability to trust yourself. Integrity requires you to do what you say you will do, without the need for a contract or promise, because of your level of integrity. Surrender to living intentionally in your new story from a place of honor, integrity, transparency, and honesty by remembering the *You* that you have always been.

Whatever pain you have experienced in your life has allowed you the development and courage to survive. Courage is the strength to face the difficult, dangerous, and frightening places and spaces in life. There are three ways to overcome every problem: force your way through, flow through by surrendering and accepting, or be ambivalent and do nothing. Forcing your way through is destructive. It is pure ego. It is the ultimate, "I'll fix this." Forcing is a masculine energy that rarely is necessary. There is a moment in every situation when decisions have to be made and force can be used effectively. On a day-to-day basis, however, a more subtle energy is needed that takes a tremendous amount of courage to summon and engage. Surrender and accept each experience as an opportunity to heal the hurt in order to re-member and reconnect to that Love. It takes courage to be willing to be authentic, speak your truth, and love unconditionally when you are so used to living with scarcity and separateness. Ultimately, allowing yourself to be vulnerable in your authenticity is the most courageous thing you can do. It takes courage to stay willing to reconnect over and over again. Whether you were aware or not, you have already woven courage into your being. Now, be aware of living courageously.

Surrender. In surrendering to Love, you wake, becoming mindful and willing to co-create. You release the wanting, needing, and desiring when you surrender and you shift your intention to that of the Divine. You become the conduit, witnessing the miracle of life. You get to play on a whole new level when you commit to authenticity. You no longer have to control. You can simply experience. That feels like the weight of the world lifting off you. Feel the flow.

Creating your new story is not about writing it down and expecting it to fall into place. Creating your story is about making conscious choices everyday to live intentionally. It is about taking responsibility for your life and your emotions. Live and experience the Divine qualities in yourself and everything around you. Your new story is about taking your power back from blame, shame, guilt, and expectations. You be You. Beautiful, sweet, wonderful You. Intelligent, creative, courageous You. Sexy, sensual, Divine You. Be You.

The Final Step

"Everyday I die again and again I'm reborn." U2, "Breathe"

Death. You have to die in order to live. I know that sounds insane and completely backwards, yet there it is. You began the process of death the day you were born. Every minute of every day, cells are dying and new ones are created within you. Ideas are being challenged; dying, and new ideas are being birthed. Those old stories and beliefs that kept you stuck needed to die in order for new stories and beliefs to be conceived. Know death in your heart and you will know life.

One day you will return Home. I am not talking about the place you sleep at night. You know this place in your heart. It is the place where you created your sacred contract. Throughout your life, you have glimpsed Home. You know when you feel a longing in your heart that you can't quite describe. Home is a place of such magnificent love and acceptance, something we humans aim to offer though usually fall short of the true potential. When you feel pain, it is a recognition that the unconditional Divine Love is not flowing. You become Homesick. There is a sweetness about Home, an expansiveness, a love so strong that no words in our vocabulary can possibly express it. Death allows you to be birthed Home. Until then, keep dying a thousand deaths and birthing a new, healing each pain layer until you are complete. In the times of need, sink into your heart and ask the Divine to provide a taste of Home through those Divine qualities. When those qualities are offered to you, receive them respectfully, humbly, and responsibly.

Now, when you face life's challenges, you can persevere with valor and patience. You can demonstrate courage and strength when tempted to go into those old, familiar blocked places by returning to the energy of Love, grounded in your knowledge that everything you need is in you and every place of challenge is an opportunity to heal and grow. Choosing authenticity, you effortlessly sacrifice for Love and gain wealth through generosity. You respect the interconnectedness of life. Aim for honor and integrity. Seek balance and flexibility. Choose compassion and empathy over judgment. Wisdom comes when the tests of anger, impatience, pride, and arrogance repeat enough that you finally make a different choice to break the cycle of victimhood.

Let go of the notion of needing to dominate or be dominated. It is easy to judge others, though we are all the same. Call out that very injustice when you see it and cease to participate in its insanity. As you meet your needs, you start to see how the painful behavior of others is simply unmet needs. Explore what is at the root. Can we all work together to heal the hurt, to meet the needs, and to live together? Duality cannot exist when the essence of Love is in you and all around you. God, Allah, Jehovah, Buddha, The Universe, Elaha, Ehyeh, Brahman, Krisna, Gitche Manitou, Ek Onkar, Jesus, Father, the Great Mathematician, whatever you call that higher being, is in all of us. As such, how can anyone be bad or less than another? We are all Divine beings on a quest to complete our sacred contracts and help others complete theirs. Surrender into that knowledge. Curiosity abounds as you seek to draw out that divinity within others, recognize it, play with it, touch Home, if only for a moment. On the other side of complexity resides simplicity. Go there.

When your raw spots are touched, feel it. Create healing. Violence is not the only way to overcome obstacles. It certainly does not further security. Touch your creativity. It's in you. Nurture it. Seek ways to bring it to life. Continue to re-story your life: Who are you today? Where are you going? What do you want? What do you need? Who do you want to be? What is your purpose today? How can you love more? How can you experience the miracle of life as the senses of the Divine? You have a choice on how you want to feel, what you want to attach to, and how you want to experience all the Divine qualities. Choose wisely, beautiful one.

Explore the meaning of things. Become a wordsmith. What is good? What is enough? What is success? What is love? Don't let me or the Merriam-Webster dictionary define it for you. Use those definitions merely as a springboard to get to your own meaning. Once you do, it holds far more weight and value. Step into unknown lands with child-like curiosity. Explore. Risk vulnerability as a way to live strong and courageously. The long journey Home begins with the first step. Grace. Salvation. Liberation. Taste it, feel it, live it!

You are so much more than you think you are and, even when you start to glimpse at your greatness, you still have so much more. When you see the beauty, strength, courage, wisdom, compassion, inspiration, humor, intelligence, and creativity in others that touches you deeply, you have witnessed a reflection of your own soul. It works in reverse, too, when you see a reflection of your shadow qualities in others. Live up to your greatness. When you say yes to that, your soul will guide you when you stray from the path, people will be brought to teach you, and more lessons will be presented to help you learn. When you see greatness in front of you, engage it. Do not fear rejection ever again. Love yourself enough that others feel it spilling out of you. Live unapologetically authentic. Go for your dreams no matter how big or impossible they seem in this moment.

You are going to fail again and again and again. *That is okay.* There are times when I can see it happening in myself, like watching an impending train wreck in slow motion. Whoops! Here are the old shadow friends again trying to help harmonize my limitations back into the energy of Love. Even if you learned the lesson of the previous failure, you probably have more layers buried below that need to heal from the same lesson. Sucks, I know. It is what it is.

Surrender. Get used to it and get efficient at recognizing it and healing.

My hope is that this book has evoked, liberated, and sustained innovation in your ability to feel *and* think, a re-membering of your wholeness, the energy of Love, and the essence that makes you so beautifully you. I wrote this for you to remind you how much you are needed, how much you are loved, how lucky this world is to have you. Now… step up, my friend. Stop letting the little child who was hurt so long ago rule your life. You are an adult. You have choices. You have power. You have love. You have wisdom. Use them! You don't have time to shirk back, play small, and just get by. There are big battles ahead. We need each other. Open your arms, eyes, heart, and mind. Shout "Yes!" to life and accept the invitation for the big adventure that awaits you.

Appendix A

FEELINGS: This is a general list of feelings. Obviously there are variations of all of these. Use the list to start identifying your feelings. If you are not finding the exact feeling, follow your heart toward anything not listed that contains energy for you in that moment.

absorbed	disappointed	involved	self-conscious
affection	disconnecte	irritated	sensitive
agony	discouraged	jealous	shocked
alert	disgusted	kindness	shy
amazed	distant	lethargic	startled
ambivalent	distracted	listless	stimulated
amused	dread	lonely	surprised
angry	eager	lost	suspicious
animated	edgy	loving	sympathy
animosity	elated	melancholy	tenderness
annoyed	embarrassed	miserable	tired
anxious	empowered	nervous	troubled
apathetic	encouraged	nostalgic	trusting
appalled	energetic	numb	turbulent
appreciative	engrossed	open	uncomfortable
apprehensive	enthusiastic	optimistic	uneasy
aroused	excited	overwhelmed	unnerved
ashamed	exhausted	pain	unsettled
astonished	expectant	passionate	upset
blissful	fascinated	peaceful	vibrant
bored	flustered	panicked	wary
burnt out	fragile	proud	withdrawn
calm	frustrated	quiet	wonder
camaraderie	grateful	radiant	worried
centered	grief	regretful	warmth
cold	guarded	relaxed	
compassion	guilty	relieved	
confident	happy	rejuvenated	
confused	hate	renewed	
contempt	hesitant	resentful	
content	heartbroken	reserved	
curious	hopeless	rested	
depleted	hurt	restless	
depressed	impatient	sad	
despair	insecure	safe	
despondent	inspired	satisfied	
detached	interested	scared	
devastated	intrigued	secure	

Infinite love + gratitude

There are so many people that have played a role in getting this book into your hands. It is impossible for me to name them all. Some had small roles in teaching me the tools I needed to heal myself. Others had a larger role in my journey by reminding me why I am lovable. For every single person who made a contract with me to come here and play with limitations and illusions in order to experience the totality of the Divine qualities, I am forever grateful.

For my many editors, especially Cindy Dick and Michael Chocise Young, wow x 7. You both made me face my limitations and fears through the "sea of red ink" and have made me a better writer. For all of the others like Anel, Belen, Adam, Laura, George, Kim, David, April, Susan, Denny (I know I am forgetting someone), your faith and investment in me is humbling.

For my "biggest fans" who without them, I could not do what I do so well. My mother and father. I know you don't always "get me" yet you always love me. Thank you. This particular book and the journey I took in writing it allowed my parents and I to resolve old hurts and evolve to a whole new lightness of being. Thank you for playing! For Angela, who for over 30 years has "had my back," thank you for getting me out of my head when I needed it most this year, for the soft landing space, and for introducing me to the one person who I owe the greatest thanks to... Dave, your love, support, morning hugs and laughter breaks allowed me the freedom to write this. It took so much longer than I expected (and so much less time than you expected). Thank you for believing in me even when you couldn't wrap your head around it, maybe especially for that part. I am blessed by the people who love me.

For all the people who have journeyed with me, providing an opportunity for me to receive the tools I needed to help you in your healing and thus, ultimately my healing, thank you. It's been an honor and a pleasure.

And finally, thank YOU for reading this book. There are many books on healing and there is truly no single process for that journey. I appreciate your time that you took to read this, for sharing the wisdom with people you recognize could use it, and for your support. I look forward to witnessing the evolution!

namaste,

ABOUT THE AUTHOR

Wendy Reese is passionate about helping people re-member "home", their essence, and how to play in their field of infinite possibilities. To learn more, please visit www.wholebeinginc.com.

Proof

23551799R00099

Made in the USA
Charleston, SC
25 October 2013